I0062611

The Complete Guide to Money Management

Proven Strategies To Get Out Of Debt, Save, Invest And Grow Your Wealth So That You Can Become Financially Free

By Joel Jacobs

"The Complete Guide To Money Management: Proven Strategies To Get Out Of Debt, Save, Invest And Grow Your Wealth So That You Can Become Financially Free". Witten by "Joel Jacobs".

The Complete Guide To Money Management is a bundle of the books "Budget Management for Beginners", "Investing For Beginners" & "Passive Income – Beginners Guide".

Hope You Enjoy!

Table of Contents

Budget Management for Beginners

Investing For Beginners

Passive Income – Beginners Guide

Budget Management for Beginners

Proven Strategies to Revamp Business & Personal Finance Habits. Stop Living Paycheck to Paycheck, Get Out of Debt, and Save Money for Financial Freedom.

Joel Jacobs

Take Control of Your Future

Money makes the world go around, but it can also leave your stomach turning. The best way to take control of your future is to take control of your finances.

Irrespective of what has happened in your past, you are standing at a crossroads. The decision that lies before you seems quite simple—do I carry on with my current trajectory or do I take the steps now necessary to secure my future financially? The mere fact that you have spent your hard-earned money on this book means that you are on the verge of choosing the latter, but probably not 100% sure yet how to get started. I am not going to lie to you—the journey you are about to embark on will not be easy. You will need to unlearn every single bad habit that you have been carrying with you from your childhood.

It is very likely that the bad money habits you have now were picked up from past generations, and if you don't make the change now, you will pass it on to future generations. From the onset of this book, you should know that the common bad habits you will need to drop include: not having a budget, overspending, running up debt, and spending little bits of money every day on small luxuries.

In order to avoid living paycheck to paycheck, you will need to find a strategy that works for you. Success won't be immediate—it will take time to break the bad habits from the past and to set yourself up for the future. You will need to find a balance between paying for the past, planning for the future, and living in the now.

The objective of this book is to provide you with the basic skills that will empower you to manage your money better. Managing money is actually not complex—you just need to learn how to cover your current expenses, have something set aside for a rainy day, and plan for the future.

When starting out on this new journey, you will need to make decisions about the following aspects related to your finances:

- Cash management
- Investments
- Family protection
- Retirement planning
- Estate planning

During the course of this book, we will briefly look at the first four aspects, but we will not delve into estate planning. (Estate planning is a specialty field and deals with how your assets will be managed once you are dead or if you become incapacitated.) The objective of this book is to provide you with the necessary skills to avoid living from paycheck to paycheck, in order for you to live a life that is filled with breathtaking experiences and is free from anxiety brought about by living on the edge of your financial means.

Step 1—Budget

Initially, it may feel quite overwhelming to create a budget, but it is the first step you need to take in order to set yourself on the path to financial freedom.

No matter how much money you make on a monthly basis, is it *not* beyond your means to pay your debts and start saving money—if you have a well-planned budget, half the battle is already won.

Like most things in life, you will only achieve success if you follow the basic principles of planning, namely:

- Determine the current status of your finances.
- Set a target, set a due date, and determine the path to reach your target.
- Identify milestones along the way that will serve as indicators that you are still on the right path.
- Implement your plan.
- Regularly review your progress.
- Regularly review your plan.

Your budget will be the foundation of the entire process but the reviews will be the plaster that keeps everything together. Things change (life happens), your financial plan and savings targets will not be the same in five years so be willing to make changes along the way.

How to Budget

It is safe to assume that you are probably aware of what your monthly income is, so the first step in developing your budget is to determine how much money you actually spend in any given month. This might mean that you will need to write down every single expense on a daily basis in order to get an accurate picture.

Remember to include ad hoc expenses, like annual subscription fees, in your budget in order to avoid potential shortfalls when the time arrives for the expense to be realized.

You will need to capture the data in a sheet—use either Excel or a free template from the internet. For the purpose of this exercise, we will create a fictional scenario. Let's meet Tom.

Tom is a 35-year-old single dad. He earns $8,500 per month and wants to set up a college savings account for his eight-year-old son, but he currently has a monthly budget shortfall of $150. He uses his credit card to cover the additional monthly expenses. Tom's sister is currently living with him, rent-free, as he needs additional help every second Saturday when he goes to work. She makes no financial contribution to the household even though she earns more than Tom on a monthly basis. Below is a list of all Tom's monthly expenses.

- *Rent $2000 (including utilities)*
- *Groceries $2000*
- *Gym membership $150 (he hasn't been to the gym in the past 4 years)*
- *Vehicle upkeep and fuel $450*
- *Cable $150*
- *School-related expenses $350*
- *Credit card bill $50*
- *Phone related expenses $ 150*
- *Clothing $200*
- *Entertainment $350 (this includes going to restaurants and other leisure expenses)*
- *Insurance $350*
- *Student loan $500*
- *Pet-related expenses $150*
- *Bank charges $350*
- *Financial support to his parents $1000*

Tom realized that these were his monthly expenses after carefully tracking everything over the course of one month, and doing a high-level review of the major expenses from previous months.

Once you (and Tom) have made a summary of all anticipated and unanticipated major expenses, the next step will be to evaluate what your long-term financial goals are. Do you want to be debt-free in three years? Buy your own house? Go on a Greek holiday? Retire comfortably?

For Tom, his priorities are to start an emergency fund (the last emergency trip to the veterinarian cost him over $500) and to start saving for his son to go to a good college one day. Tom's sister also advised that he may need to start putting money away towards his retirement if he doesn't want his son to have to take care of him one day—as he now has to help take care of his parents.

In order for Tom to be able to afford all these long-term goals, he will need to find at least $1000 per month extra. He won't be able to generate other sources of income, so he will need to reduce his expenses—but where to begin?

If you are in the same position as Tom and you need to find a way to cut your expenses, the best place would be to start by figuring out which expenses are necessary (mandatory) and which are not (discretionary).

Mandatory expenses, according to Davis (2021) are those expenses that are difficult to avoid such as expenses related to:

- Housing
- Transportation
- Groceries
- Utilities
- Health care
- Child care
- Debt
- Savings

Davis (2021) lists the following as discretionary expenses which more often than not are the budget items where savings can be found:

- Foods and drinks prepared outside the home
- Clothing and accessories
- Cosmetics and personal products
- Electronics
- Alcohol and tobacco
- Gifts
- Entertainment
- Travel

Based on the two lists above, it is very likely that Tom may have forgotten some expenses and that he is actually overspending much more frequently than he originally calculated, meaning that his debt burden may be larger than he actually anticipates.

Honesty is the foundation of the budgeting process, and if you are not honest about where your money is going, you are never going to find the source of your spending problems.

It might sound a bit harsh, but in all likelihood, the main factor in your current situation of living from paycheck to paycheck (or even worse from paycheck to debt to paycheck) is spending too much money on discretionary items.

Cutting Expenses / Increasing Your Income

After you have gone through the budgeting process, you may very well realize that you are either spending up to the very last cent of your income, or you may even have reached a point where you are increasing your debt burden by using your credit card as a secondary 'income'. If you are living beyond your income, it is also very likely that you are not building up your savings. If you are in this space, you will need to start cutting back on expenses.

Below are a few tips to consider in order to reduce your monthly expenses:

- Cut back on your energy bill.
- Reduce your grocery bill.
- Prioritize paying off your debt.
- Adjust your cell phone or cable bill to avoid overage fees.
- Avoid trips to restaurants, bars, and coffee shops.
- Plan your trips to the grocery store.
- Avoid expensive hobbies.
- Find free opportunities for exercise and entertainment.
- Pay your debt on time.
- Cancel monthly subscriptions.

Part of the budgeting process also entails that you keep yourself accountable for your expenses. The only way to do this is to capture your daily expenses and track them against the amount you budgeted for them every month. Once you have reached the limit of your budget, then you can no longer have any expenditure in that category.

An easy example—you love sushi and have included $100 per month for sushi in your budget. You get your salary on the 1st of the month, your friend has their birthday on the 5th and you all go out for dinner at your favorite sushi restaurant. By the end of the evening, you are a few drinks strong and declare vehemently that you are paying for everyone—the final bill is $150. Not only have you spent your entire sushi budget at the beginning of the month, you now need to cut spending on another budget line item as well. So for the remainder of the month, you are not allowed to have your favorite treat.

In order to determine whether or not an expense is warranted, ask yourself one simple question—do I want it, or do I need it?

Going back to Tom, his options in terms of cutting expenses are to:

- Cancel his gym membership.
- Calculate how much a babysitter would cost him twice a month compared to his sister living permanently with

them (taking into consideration the additional grocery and utility expenses).

- Reduce his entertainment budget.
- Reduce his clothing budget.
- Put a limit on the amount of time his son can spend on the phone.

You might reach a point where you are no longer able to cut your expenses, but you still need to create more cash. Apart from robbing a bank (don't rob a bank), the only other alternatives for generating more cash is to expand your income stream. This can be done by starting a business on the side, by getting a second job, or by selling unnecessary goods.

Step 2—Fight the Debt Trap

Americans owed more than $1 trillion in credit card debt alone, with a significant jump in debt occurring during the holiday season. 75% of individuals who had credit card debt at the start of 2020 indicated that they would not be able to repay those debts before interest would be charged (Epperson & Dickler, 2020).

Debt is a significant hurdle on the road to reaching your financial goals. If you are in debt, you are less likely to be able to build up any discernible savings and you will be forced to decide whether to prioritize debt repayment or saving.

Some of the advantages of prioritizing debt repayment on your journey towards financial freedom include:

- Reducing the overall cost of your debt by reducing the amount of interest paid over time.
- Improving your credit score.
- Enabling you to focus on savings and other financial goals once you are debt-free.
- Removing the emotional burden associated with debt.
- Enabling you to free up money to invest in experiences that you enjoy.
- Avoiding the threat of losing everything when life goes around an unexpected corner because you are able to own your assets.

Why Debt Is More Expensive Than You Think

Debt is sometimes more expensive than we anticipate because we often forget about the interest added to any debt incurred. Let's quickly do a bit of math to better understand the crux of the problem—here is our fictional friend Tom again to create our next scenario:

Tom owes $1,000 on his credit card, with an annual interest rate of 18% charged on the debt. He has one of two options available to him—Option 1 is paying only the minimum amount payable, which is $50 per month. Option 2 is to pay $100 per month. How much will his debt cost him at the end of the day?

It might seem as if Option 1 would be the preferred option because he will only need to pay $50 every month, but over time his debt will cost him more than $100 more to repay over a longer period of time. With the interest rate at 18% per year, it will take Tom two years to repay the debt, with an additional $197.83 paid in interest. If Tom chooses Option 2, he will only need eleven months to repay his debt, with the interest amounting to $91.62 only.

Therefore, by opting to pay off his debt in a shorter period of time, he ultimately saves $106.20 and is debt-free thirteen months earlier than if he only opted for the minimum amount payable.

The Devil Is in the Details

When it comes to debt, make sure that you check the details. In other words—study your bill on a monthly basis, and make sure you understand the fine print on any debt you incur.

Always check your bill—mistakes can be made or people can deliberately try to defraud you, so always make sure that you go through whatever bill you need to pay to ensure that it is the right amount and includes the cost of only the services rendered. By doing this, you not only avoid paying for something that you don't have to pay for, but you also start getting a better understanding of how your debt is put together—especially the amount of interest you need to pay or any penalties that might occur if the debt is not settled in time.

The fine print of a contract is all the important information that is excluded from the main body of the document and is often included as either addendums or footnotes. Information that the document issuer does not want you to pay attention to, but should actually know, is normally hidden in the fine print.

Most people may don't consider reading the fine print as important as reading the instructions. But at least with instructions, you can still retrace your steps, and fish the box from the trash—once you sign any form of loan or credit agreement there is no going back.

Though some of the costs related to the fine print may seem insignificant at first, a lot of small expenses tend to accumulate over time and can be as devastating to your cash flow as single large expenditures.

Here are a few steps you can take in order to protect yourself when it comes to contractual legalese:

- Take time to review the documents and ask questions about clauses that you do not understand.
- Seek the advice of legal experts, especially in instances where you are incurring major debts.
- When buying anything "as is", get a second opinion on the condition of the item you are purchasing before you sign the final documentation, in order to avoid buying yourself a hole in your pocket.

Debt Repayment Strategies

In order to get out of debt, you need to have a strategy as well as a deadline for when you want to be debt-free.

If you have more than one source of debt, one strategy might be to prioritize which debt is settled first. Though you will need to try and make some sort of payment on all the debt you face, it is best to settle debts with higher interest rates or those with penalties attached to them first in order to reduce the overall cost of your debt over time.

Another strategy to consider would be to focus first on repaying smaller debts first, as settling those debts might bring about a sense of accomplishment that will keep you motivated to pay off the remaining debts.

A third option to consider is borrowing money to pay off all other debts, in order to have only one monthly payment. These types of loans are called debt consolidation loans. Before you opt for this strategy make sure that this consolidated loan will still cost you less per month than the gradual repayment of your separate debts.

At the end of the day, however, you will need to find the strategy that works best for you and stick with it.

Whatever strategy you end up choosing, the following tips can come in handy along your debt repayment journey:

- Make a list of all your debt and write down how much it actually costs you every month.
- Reduce living expenses in order to increase the gap between money in and money out, thus freeing up more cash to either save or pay debt.
- Constantly monitor your progress.

Good Debt

Student and mortgage loans have generally been considered "good debt", as in both instances you owe money on something that can help you earn more money over time or improve your life in important ways. However, considering the current global economy, the only good debt is the debt you have already paid off.

Though a student loan provides you with a degree that can potentially increase your earning ability, and a mortgage means that you have invested in an asset, both can go horribly wrong if you do not read the market correctly.

In the current economic conditions, the likelihood that any new entrant into the job market will be guaranteed a gradually increasing income and job security will be very low for at least the next five years. Therefore, if you are heading towards tertiary education in the next two years, you should try to avoid debt as much as possible. In a few years, however, the world will look much more different and the situation could be a lot better. So the point that you should take away from this is to evaluate the current and potential economic markets to determine if you will be able to afford your debt within the foreseeable future.

The same holds true for mortgages—if you borrow more than you can afford, do not fully understand the terms and conditions of your mortgage, or are investing in a property market that is in the midst of a downward spiral, you are likely to lose your family home to foreclosure. When you borrow money to procure your first home, make sure that you understand how much it is that you can borrow (generally not more than 28% of your gross monthly income) and pay attention to what the housing market is doing at that time.

Nearly 10% of Americans can be considered "house poor", meaning they have taken out mortgages on homes they cannot afford and then end up being unable to cover other expenses, optimize savings opportunities, or invest for future endeavors (Brennan, 2020).

When it comes to debt, don't ask what you can do for your debt, ask what your debt can do for you—or in other words, make sure that if you do incur debt it is for something that can actually improve your wealth in the future, but don't incur debt if you will not be able to afford it.

How to Avoid Debt

Debt that should be avoided at all costs is any debt you may incur when purchasing something that loses its value over time, or which is consumed within a short period of time. This includes debts related to vehicles, clothes and consumables, and holidays. Taking out payday loans and using credit cards for these types of purchases means that the final cost of these items can easily be in excess of 200% higher than the initial cost, due to penalties and exorbitant interest rates.

Before you enter into new debt, ask yourself the following questions:

- Does the debt make sense taking into consideration how much you would need to repay?
- Will you be able to recover almost all your money or even more through the purpose of the debt?
- Are there better options available to you to utilize the money that will actually contribute to your future financial security?

Most young Americans have a significant debt burden to deal with once they leave college—due to student loans. In order to avoid starting out far below zero when you enter the job market, try to avoid taking out student loans that will exceed in total what you are likely to earn in your first year being employed.

Other tips which may prove useful in avoiding an increased debt burden while in the process of repaying existing debts include:

- Avoid purchases that you cannot afford without going into debt.
- Cut up your credit card—if you don't have it, you can't use it.
- Pay daily living expenses with cash. A good technique for providing a bit of a spending reality check is to put all funds to be used for living expenses in an envelope and use the

envelope for all payments. This way, you can literally see the money flow from your pocket

- Ignore friends and family who are overspending—you can provide them with advice on how to improve their own financial position, but you are not obliged to provide them with financial assistance if it means that you will not be able to pay your dues.
- Say no to unnecessary outings and expenses.
- Pay your debts on time and avoid additional penalties and fees.

Step 3 - Don't Keep up with the Jones's

"Keeping up with the Jones's" is an idiom that stems from the early 1900s and refers to the constant conscious or subconscious comparison you might be making between your lifestyle and those of your peers. This behavior often results in a feeling of inadequacy that could eventually translate into debt if you actively attempt to copy those you measure yourself against. Your story is not their story and it will always be best to live below your means since whoever you are trying to impress will not pay your debts.

Going into debt in order to fund your lifestyle means that your lifestyle is unsustainable in the long run and the true cost of debt goes beyond your bank balance since overspending will have a negative influence on your mental wellbeing.

So before you swipe that credit card on something cool you saw on social media, ask yourself the following questions:

- Why do I want this?
- Do I really need it?
- How long will I use this?
- Can I afford this?

More often than not, the Jones's we are chasing are not even friends and neighbors, but strangers on social media. Their life is not your life; you don't know how much debt they have or whether or not they actually outright own any of the things they put on display (it might all very well be fake). So do yourself a favor and let the Jones's go. These steps will get you off to a good start:

- Focus on yourself and your future and follow the plan that will get you there.
- Live with gratitude.
- Enjoy life within your financial boundaries.

- Check your social media circle—some people may actually have a toxic influence on your mental wellbeing (unfollow them).

Just remember—it is highly unlikely that anybody will post their debt balloon proudly on Instagram.

Maximizing your own social media likes will also have little influence on how those who love you the most will remember you one day. The influencer lifestyle is not sustainable; rushing around, trying to draw the fickle attention of social media scrollers is not a long-term career and the likelihood that you will still have the same following five years from now is very unlikely. Though you might not be actively seeking the influencer lifestyle, you may still secretly be looking for online validation. Do not let the like of likes drag you into a pit of debt. You will not worry about the number of likes you had on a plate of food at a restaurant that you couldn't afford when you are seventy—you will, however, worry about where your next meal will come from if you did not adequately prepare for retirement.

One of the greatest investments you can make is to learn to move away from the "fear of missing out" and start embracing the "joy of missing out".

Focus on keeping up with your goals, rather than chasing the Jones's. Figure out what will be important to you ten years from now, and chase that. Find ways to create your own happiness—you are the only person that can influence how happy you are. Let others find their own path to happiness.

If you want to buy happiness, focus on purchases that will translate into experiences, will be an unexpected treat for yourself or someone else, will make life a bit easier by increasing your free time, will delay gratification, or are an investment in somebody else's success.

Step 4 – Plan for a Rainy Day

You don't know what you don't know, so it is best to plan for the unknown.

Paying off debts is one of the key strategies to execute if you want to ensure future financial stability, but you still need to find a balance between living, paying off debt, and saving money.

Though debt repayment should always be a priority on your journey towards financial freedom, getting into the savings game early also holds some advantages, such as:

- The longer you can save, the more time compound interest has to work its magic.
- Being able to work towards other goals earlier, rather than having to wait for debt to be repaid.
- Avoiding future debt by having an emergency fund available when the unexpected happens.

The debt trap can sneak up on you incrementally or can rush in from left field and tackle you off your feet—that is where planning for a rainy day comes into the picture. Paying off your debt is important, but having an emergency fund is just as important, as it is one of the best ways to avoid going into severe debt suddenly.

The idiom "to save money for a rainy day" has been around for well over 500 years and usually refers to setting money aside in order to satisfy a need in the future. Over the past few years GoFundMe campaigns have been used by many as a way to fund emergency expenses, but you cannot rely on the goodness of friends and strangers to dig you out of unforeseen expenses—especially medical expenses—on a regular basis. Eventually, goodwill will run out and you will need to keep your financial boat afloat by yourself.

So before you have to rely on charity to pay major expenses, start setting up an emergency fund for that rainy day.

How Much Is Enough

Financial advisors generally recommend that your emergency fund be substantial enough to cover three to six months' worth of personal expenses. It will take some time to get there, but don't stop putting money into your emergency fund once you have reached your initial target. You will never regret having too much money in your "rainy day" account, but you will always regret not having enough.

If the day does come that you need to dip into your emergency funds, be sure to replace whatever you took out, as you may be faced with another emergency sooner than anticipated.

When setting up your emergency fund, make sure that the money is accessible but not so easily accessible that you are tempted to use it for splurges here and there. The easier it is for you to access your emergency fund, the more likely it is that you might dip into the fund for non-emergency reasons. Try to find a savings option that will ensure access to the funds within at least three days, but that could potentially also earn dividends or accumulate good interest over time. You should also avoid high-risk investments when considering various options for investing, as you do not want to face the possibility of lost investments when you are already facing another emergency.

In some instances, setting up a reasonable nest egg might need to be prioritized over paying off debt, especially in circumstances with a high probability of significant unforeseen expenses, or if job security is not guaranteed.

The final decision between whether you should focus on savings or debt repayment will be based on your own personal financial goals.

Is Insurance Necessary?

Taking out, or having insurance, refers to the process of paying scheduled fees to an insurance company in order to be able to reclaim money from them in the event of harm befalling a person or object. Insurance coverage can be obtained to cover damages related to property and assets, health care, and/or death.

The three most important insurance types currently available on the market include life insurance, health insurance, and liability insurance. It is best to go over the type of insurance and total coverage required with a qualified professional. Spending money on insurance when you are hardly getting by on your current salary may seem unnecessary, but the long-term benefits will outweigh the short-term costs.

Below are a few reasons why having insurance is beneficial:

- It can ensure your family's financial stability in the event of an emergency.
- It brings peace of mind to know that some of the most significant expenses for your family will be covered in the event of an untimely death or incapacitation.
- It can be used as a tax break.
- It can improve the probability of qualifying for a home or business loan.

The younger you are when you buy insurance, the cheaper it will be. Insurance companies use some serious math to calculate your risk profile and younger people tend to have a better risk profile, this is lifestyle dependent, however.

In early 2020, nearly a third of all working Americans had some kind of medical debt. On average, Americans spent in excess of $5,000 per year on out-of-pocket health care, which can include the cost of medical insurance, but also includes costs related to medication and medical supplies (Leonhardt, 2020). Each year many people are left without medical insurance at a time when they need it most. This results in an escalating debt crisis, as many people avoid going for medical treatment, but then end up with even more significant costs later on when the problem has escalated.

If you are currently in a situation where you have little or no medical insurance and rising medical debts, you probably do not even want to have a conversation about any type of insurance—you just want to get out of debt before your debt is sent for collection and you end up becoming part of the growing number of Americans that have been forced into bankruptcy as a result of unpayable medical expenses.

Before you become completely despondent about the medical debt mountain in front of you, just remember that most service providers will be satisfied with having debts settled over a period of time, as opposed to not having the debt settled at all. Therefore, try to negotiate a debt payment plan or seek the advice of a medical billing advocate to help you negotiate your current reality.

Planning for Retirement

Retirement planning is essential to ensure that you can be financially independent and able to respond to whatever life throws at you at a time in your life when your earning potential has shrunk to zero. In your twenties, it may seem like an absolutely ridiculous idea to start planning for retirement, but the younger you are when you start thinking about the day that you are old, the better it will work out for you in the end. When planning for retirement, you will need to anticipate possible living expenses as well as medical expenses.

When you plan for your retirement the financial component is critical, but you should not lose sight of the quality of life component as well. Retirement is the time when you should be able to enjoy all the hard work you have put in, and whether that means being able to take a nap whenever you want or travel the world with your friends, your planning should be done in such a way that you have sufficient resources in order to attain the quality of life you aspire to in retirement.

We have listed below some more reasons as to why retirement planning is important.

- Most countries have a maximum age at which you can no longer seek formal employment.
- People are living longer than before, so retirement funds will need to last longer as well.
- The older you get, the more likely you are to develop medical emergencies.
- Having only one source of income when you retire can be very risky—especially if it is funded by the government.
- Your children cannot be used as your retirement plan.

The process of retirement planning can be described—in a nutshell—as the process of setting income goals for retirement and identifying the actions that will need to be executed in order to achieve those goals. It is generally recommended to plan for having access to between 70% - 90% of your pre-retirement income in order to live a good life.

The best time to start planning for retirement is the moment you start working, but even if you are a few years behind, don't fret. Start planning and investing in your retirement now—better late, than never.

Planning for your retirement is not brain surgery, but you may require professional assistance along the way to provide you with all the information you may need in order to make decisions about:

- The age at which you want to retire.
- Potential future expenses based on current expenses and potential future changes in circumstances.
- The best portfolio mix that takes into consideration your goals.

- The best options to make up for lost time.

Living within your means and saving money can often seem like a tedious task, so one of the easiest ways to trick yourself into saving money is to ensure that whatever you are planning on saving is already out of your account and into your investment before you even realize it is gone.

Some employers have savings programs at work—talk to the relevant persons within your workplace and find out whether or not your company has such a program and whether or not you qualify for it. Just make sure you read the fine print and that the savings program aligns with your needs. Try to maximize the amount of money you can invest in such a program, especially if there is the option of the employer matching whatever the employee contributes up to a maximum amount.

If you create a retirement fund outside your work environment, avoid using the money you have set aside for retirement for other purposes. The money must be left undisturbed for as long as possible in order to maximize the benefits of compound interest.

The Beauty of Compound Interest

Compound interest is the interest you receive on not only the original capital invested, but also on the interest that you have accumulated throughout the duration of your savings. Basically, it is interest on interest (Fernando, 2019). With any investment or savings you are likely to generate interest, but compound interest will ensure that your invested amount will grow faster than simple interest.

When you are investing money, always look for compound interest; when you are taking out a loan, always try to avoid compound interest.

Let's talk about Tom again.

Tom repaid his debt in eleven months and opted to create a savings fund for his son (who is currently eight years old) with the $91.62 that he originally saved on his credit card debt. He is planning on saving for ten years at a fixed interest rate of 5%, with an additional monthly payment of $50 to the investment. With compound interest added on an annual basis, Tom's son will have $7,695.97 in his savings fund by the time he turns eighteen years old. Tom contributed $6,091.62, while earning $ 1,604.35 in interest. If Tom's son continues saving at the same rate as his father until he is forty years old, he would have a savings fund of $45,615.86, of which $19,291.62 was contributed by Tom and his father, and $26,324.24 was earned through compound interest.

In order to experience the full benefit of earning any form of interest on your savings or investments, you will need to remain patient. Interest accumulates over time, and the more time you have available to wait, the bigger the return will be. That is why it is of critical importance to start saving as soon as possible—especially if you want to be prepared for a rainy day.

Step 5 – Speak to an Expert

"A good plan violently executed now is better than a perfect plan next week," – General George S Patton

Though it seems a bit brutal to look at inspiration from a World War II General when it comes to financial planning, General Patton understood the risks of getting stuck in your own mind and "analysis paralysis". Often when we need to make difficult decisions about our own lives, we get overwhelmed with all the information that we need to sort and analyze and never get to a point where we can make a decision and execute it effectively.

Figuring out the best plan for yourself and your family can be daunting, especially if you are under a significant debt burden. Finding the light at the end of the tunnel can seem like a nearly impossible event, and the mounting pressures can start to create significant anxiety. If you ever find yourself in such a situation, it is best to find a qualified expert to offer guidance regarding which options are available to you.

A qualified financial advisor can help you to evaluate your financial needs and can assist with a variety of aspects related to the financial realm—like advice on investments or clarification of tax laws.

Before you engage with any person that claims to be an advisor, ensure that they are registered with the relevant authorities in your area. Do your research before you trust.

Below is a list of potential experts that you can seek guidance from:

- Brokers: Brokers will suggest a selection of investment or insurance products that they deem valuable for you based on your specific goals. These individuals may not necessarily be bound to a fiduciary standard and may at times oversell you on what you need.

- Independent/fee-only advisors: Advisors offer a broader service, so they will be able to provide insight into almost all aspects of personal financial management such as budgeting, estate planning, debt repayment, and much more. They may either be linked to a broker and be paid commission for products they sell (Independent advisor) or work as a fee-only advisor, obtaining payment from the investments they recommend.
- Planners: Financial planners are the ones you need to engage with when it comes to figuring out how you can turn a little money into a lot, over time. They help you set up a financial plan that will work for you and your family based on your current and potential future needs.
- Money coaches: If you are unsure of what your goals should be, a money coach might be the answer to your problems. They help you see the big picture and can suss out what your objectives are even before you are able to articulate them.
- Debt counselors: In the event that your debt has reached uncontrollable levels, debt counselors may just be the answer to your prayers. They can help you set up a plan that will work for you—that allows you to still have a semblance of a life—while still paying off your debts. They may even be able to negotiate a repayment plan with lower interest rates and reduced penalties.
- Investment advisors: These individuals can only provide advice on an investment strategy as well as the potential investments to consider. Make sure that you choose an advisor that is not under obligation to sell a certain amount of investments on a monthly basis.
- Accountants: Accountants are often the butt of jokes in the media, but they play a vital role in ensuring that you remain solvent and on the right side of tax services.

Never feel ashamed to ask for help. Not everybody can be an expert in everything and, though Google is an awesome tool, you may still need to consult with a trained professional in order to figure out the final details of what you need and how you are going to get there.

Just remember—expert advice will not come cheaply but in the end, it can be a great investment for your own future. Make sure that you can afford the expense of going to an advisor because it is of little value to engage with a financial management expert if the whole process of consultation is beyond your financial means.

Knowing when to engage with an expert is half the battle, but the general consensus is that you should seek expert advice under the following circumstances: you are within five years of retiring, you have reached a milestone like buying a house or being accepted to university, or your income has suddenly increased.

When looking for somebody to assist you in setting up a long-term plan for you and your family, do your research—don't go to the first person recommended by an acquaintance of an acquaintance. Try to avoid individuals that work on a commission basis only, and remember, if it is too good to be true, it is probably a scam. Unfortunately, when it comes to proper financial management and planning, slow and steady is the only sustainable approach to follow.

Though there is no law that prevents it, it tends to be best not to turn to your friends or family even though they may be qualified financial advisors. You will need to take emotion out of the process which will not always be easy when you are too familiar with your advisor. You will need somebody that can be objective and strict during the planning process and a friend or family member might try to spare your feelings, while you will not have that luxury with a stranger.

It can, however, be daunting to rely on the advice of a complete stranger when it comes to your future, so do some research about whether or not financial advisors need to be registered with an external body in your country. Though it is not a guarantee that you will not be scammed, there is at least still some comfort in the fact that the person helping you plan for your future can be held accountable by a legal entity.

Once you have had a conversation with your advisor, remember one thing—it is still your money. You don't have to feel bad if you want a second opinion. Don't be forced into making a decision that you are not yet comfortable with or sign contracts if you are not sure of the hidden costs and commissions involved. You have the right to ask questions—whether you earn $1,000 per month or $100,000.

Initially, you may feel a bit underprepared to have a meeting with an advisor, since you may not understand a lot of the complexities of financial markets and financial management. There is, however, a simple hack for overcoming this barrier—follow the right people online.

Like we previously said—don't just trust one opinion, as there will never be just one resource that will cover the complexities of your personal experience. Diversify your sources of information and listen to different points of view.

Providing a comprehensive list of individuals to learn from on social media platforms would be near impossible, but try to avoid anybody that sells themself as an "influencer". A timeless approach to getting a quick list to sort through would be to ask your preferred search engine for a list of financial experts to follow online.

Though these online experts will not replace the value of talking to an advisor, engaging with them from afar will help broaden your personal knowledge base and put you on the path to greater understanding.

Technology can also be a valuable tool to track your spending or savings. There are a great number of apps currently available that can help you track your daily spending, adherence to your budget, and progress towards your savings goals.

It may seem to be a bit excessive to track your daily spending or to check in on the progress towards your savings goals on a regular basis, but it can also serve as a needed reality check and a silent accountability partner on this new journey towards financial freedom.

Step 6 – Save Now, Spend Later

Under most circumstances, people will have a savings account for one of three reasons:

- To have sufficient money in case of an emergency.
- To reduce the amount of money needed when applying for a loan.
- To have a bit of fun by spoiling themselves with something a bit extravagant.

We have already covered saving for a rainy day, so now we will spend some time on the other two reasons—taking money from yourself today so your future self can have some fun later and putting away savings in order to reduce your debt burden when you do need a loan in future. It is especially important to know how long you have to invest, as that will also have an influence on the type of investments you would consider.

While having an emergency fund and a retirement fund is great, you actually want to live life in the here and now as well. It is good to have long-term savings, but you can also set up a "splash" fund for things such as holidays or new electronics—anything that gives you joy outside the everyday drudgery. Such items will normally be part of your short-term savings plan that should cover larger planned expenses that will occur within the next two years.

You can even start building savings for bigger ticket items such as a home or a new car. Though you may not be able to save enough to buy either of these two without debt, it can make debt a lot smaller if you start saving now to at least reduce the size of the loan. These items are normally incorporated into your medium-term savings and should cover planned expenses that are likely to occur within the next five to 10 years.

Whether or not you are establishing a short or medium-term saving, the principles will remain the same —have a budget and have a plan.

Once you have settled your debts and have built up a bit of savings, you can let your hair hang loose by including line items in your budget for monthly treats, like a trip to your favorite fancy restaurant or a few new books.

Avoiding impulse buys

The one habit you need to break to ensure that you can maintain the momentum that you have built up is impulse buying.

Impulse buying is often triggered by emotions and results in the purchase of goods and services without planning the purchase in advance. This behavior can either be triggered by anxiety and unhappiness or can result in anxiety and unhappiness; therefore, reduced psychological well-being can either be a cause of financial problems or can be created by them.

Impulse buyers frequently share some characteristics, such as:

- Being status-conscious and image-concerned, and therefore like to look good in the eyes of others.
- Having high levels of anxiety and difficulty controlling emotions.
- Having low happiness levels and looking towards shopping for a short-term high brought about by the spending spree endorphin rush.
- Not thinking about the long-term consequences of their actions—just looking for the instant gratification offered by impulse buying.

According to Cruze (2020), the average American spends over $5000 annually on impulse buys. This translates to just over $400 per month and if this monthly expenditure was put into a savings account (even at minimal interest rates) it would be worth over $25,000 after only five years. You are therefore losing a significant potential investment opportunity—all thanks to unhealthy emotions.

In order to break the habit of impulse buying, make the following behaviors part of your daily habits:

- Stick to your budget.
- Allow yourself some opportunity to spend—just make sure this line item on your budget is reasonable and affordable.
- Take time and think about the purchase before you act.
- Don't go shopping without a plan.
- Don't add yourself to email lists.
- Avoid shopping when you are emotional.
- Don't shop alone.
- Leave your credit card at home.
- Stop comparing yourself to others.
- Challenge your friends to a no-spend challenge.
- Keep your goals in mind.

If you have thought about an item for a while and realize that it is something you absolutely cannot go without, create a short-term savings plan for the item by adjusting your budget in order to be able to afford it a few months down the line—with the added benefit of NO additional debt.

How to Maintain Momentum

Living within your means might be a novelty at the beginning, but after a few months of restricting yourself, you might be tempted to chuck the plan in the nearest river and go and buy yourself something nice. In order to maintain momentum, you have to make budgeting a habit, and a habit will take time. You might even need to change your thinking about money and budgets—in the end budgeting does not limit your freedom, it actually gives you the wings to fly. Once you start believing it, half the battle is won.

Changing the way you think about money will not happen overnight and you might need to do a bit of work to make the change. Below are a few tips that may help you change your money mindset:

- Read more books that will have a positive impact on your thinking.
- Be generous.
- Have a picture in mind for your retirement.
- Believe that you will achieve.

Initially, the only way to maintain momentum when it comes to this new journey of financial freedom is to take emotion and willpower out of the equation. If you have to decide on a monthly basis whether or not you are going to send $100 to a savings account, you will opt to do something fun with the money, instead of saving it.

Setting up automatic transfers means that you take the thinking out of the process, and you get used to the money just not being available anymore after a while. In this way, you ensure that saving can happen in an effortless and consistent manner.

It is also important to set goals for yourself. Goals provide you with a destination and it is easier to maintain momentum if you know what the destination is, and by when you would like to reach it.

Something else that you will need to focus on is to be present in your own life. By being more self-aware you will be able to start identifying potential triggers for the emotions that could result in an expensive shopping spree. By being able to read situations or emotions that could derail your savings train, you can learn to regulate yourself and thus potentially avoid significant, unplanned expenses.

Never lose sight of the big picture. While it is important to focus on the small victories, your destination is what will ultimately serve as the biggest motivator to not go off track. There was a reason why you decided that living from one paycheck to the next is not the final reality that you want to settle for. Never forget that "why".

Step 7 – Living generously

"What good shall I do this day?" – Benjamin Franklin

According to Livingston (n.d), happiness economists have found that giving money to help others is often one of the most rewarding ways to spend money.

Regardless of your current financial situation, try to start including a category for donations into your budget. By planning to live generously, you make it a priority instead of an afterthought. By giving, even if you think you can't afford it, you start to live outwards and move beyond selfishness while gradually becoming more aware of the needs of others. The discipline needed to accommodate even the smallest generosity when you are trying to get and stay out of debt can also serve you well in the overall practice of being responsible with your money.

You might be asking the question to yourself now—why must I be generous if I have to cut down on Starbucks or take out or other things that make me happy? Giving with an open heart and mind provides benefits beyond the instant gratification of a soy latte.

Below are some of the benefits that you may experience once you start living a more generous life:

- People who live generously have been found to have greater satisfaction with life and appear to be happier all around.
- Relationships tend to be stronger and more reciprocal in those that are considered to be generous.
- People who tend to give more easily are happier in their careers.
- Generous individuals tend to have a more positive outlook on life.
- Due to higher satisfaction levels and a more positive disposition, mental and physical health tend to be higher in those that are more generous.

- Once you start looking outwards—seeing the need of others—you become more satisfied with what you have and tend to care a lot less about "keeping up with the Jones's".
- Generous people tend to have higher self-esteem and this can be a great counter to the need for indulging in retail therapy in order to feel better about oneself.
- Generous people are often willing to work harder and will do what it takes to achieve their goals since they see their own success as not only being of benefit to them but also to others.

One of the greatest investments you can make in your future self is to learn to be more generous. Even if you cannot spare a single cent initially, you can still be generous with your time or other resources, without it costing you anything. Regardless of how you decide to live more generously, doing so will definitely change your life for the better. Once you realize that others' success will not diminish your own, a ripple effect can be created that uplifts entire communities and, the more successful those around you become, the more successful you actually become.

Generosity does have a dark side as well, especially when you give with the expectation of receiving something in return or if you have people that might look at exploiting your generosity for their own benefit. You should always give without expectation and trust that others are honest in their motivations, but remain aware of the pitfalls and re-evaluate the situation when you realize that you may be sucked into the dark side of generosity. Learn to say no without feeling bad about it.

Thinking should be part of the process of being generous. Don't force your generosity onto somebody or give because it is on your to-do list for the day. True generosity comes from a place where you have identified a need in others, and realize that you have something that could be of benefit to them.

Keep up the Good Work

The road to financial freedom will be paved with patience and declined take-out. There are no quick fixes and the only option will be to concentrate on your plan—one step at a time. Always keep an eye on how far you have come, celebrate when you reach a milestone, and keep at it.

Life would have been so much easier if we had learned more about personal financial management when we were a lot younger. One of the best investments you can make in your own future financial well-being is to ensure that your children learn financial management skills from a young age. The best way they will learn about money is by watching how you work with money, but it is important to ensure that they understand why you do things in a certain way. That understanding will only be fostered by having conversations with them and exposing them to the basic principles of budgeting at a young age.

The younger they are when they start saving, the better. The beauty of compound interest is that, even if they start saving just $10 per month at the age of eight, they will have a nice little nest egg by the time they leave school. Many parents compromise their own financial future when they have to bail out their children when their financial planning fails them; teach them young and they might not need you or your emergency fund as their emergency fund when they are older.

The basic principles for setting yourself up for financial freedom to be instilled in all children and adults are as follows:

- Have a budget.
- Stick to your budget.
- Pay your debt.
- Start building a reserve for emergencies.

Once your financial situation starts improving, you will be tempted to increase your expenditure as well. The improvement might be because you are starting to see the benefits of financial planning or might be a result of an increase in income. Whatever the reason for the extra money left over at the end of the month, try to resist the urge to splurge. Rather, increase your savings—either towards your emergency fund or towards an item that you have long dreamed about. Try to avoid splashing cash on items that will only result in instant gratification, but not in long-term satisfaction.

At the end of the day, you want your money to work for you—don't get stuck in a cycle of squirreling money away in a savings account. Yes, it is good to have money in an emergency fund, but once you become more financially mobile, start diversifying your investments in order to ensure that you have diversified exposure to risks and opportunities—the ideal is to have your money earn money without you having to do much about it.

The last thought I would like to leave you with is this—remember to give, but don't give beyond what you can afford. Society was built on the premise of people helping each other when they were in a position to do so, so try to live more generously—not only for the benefit of others but also for yourself.

References

5 Budgeting Basics to Create a Budget That Works | Discover. (2017, August 22). Discover Bank - Banking Topics Blog. https://www.discover.com/online-banking/banking-topics/5-budgeting-basics/

5.1 The Budget Process | Personal Finance. (n.d.). Courses.lumenlearning.com. https://courses.lumenlearning.com/suny-personalfinance/chapter/5-1-the-budget-process/

9 Reasons Why Retirement Planning Is Important | Pure Financial Advisors, Inc. (2018, April 6). Pure Financial Advisors, Inc. https://purefinancial.com/learning-center/blog/why-retirement-planning-is-important/

11 quotes that show the great leadership of General George Patton. (2015, December 21). Business Insider. https://www.businessinsider.com/11-quotes-that-show-the-great-leadership-of-general-george-patton-2015-11#2-a-good-plan-violently-executed-now-is-better-than-a-perfect-plan-next-week-2

25 Reasons Keeping Up With the Joneses' is a Terrible Pursuit. (2020, April 6). Home Stratosphere. https://www.homestratosphere.com/reasons-keeping-up-with-the-joneses-is-a-terrible-pursuit/

Adcock, S. (2019, May 16). *Keeping up with the Joneses? Don't - most of them are flat broke.* Think Save Retire. https://thinksaveretire.com/the-joneses-are-broke/

AES Financial Services. (n.d.). *Financial Planning Guide - Expert guidance for your financial planning.* Www.aesinternational.com. https://www.aesinternational.com/financial-planning-guide

Alvarez, J. (2020, July 20). *Good debt vs. bad debt: Why what you've been told is probably wrong.* CNBC. https://www.cnbc.com/2020/07/20/good-debt-vs-bad-debt-why-what-youve-been-told-is-probably-

wrong.html#:~:text=%E2%80%9CGood%E2%80%9D%20debt%2
0is%20defined%20as

Becker, J. (n.d.). *9 Ways Generous People See the World Differently*. Becoming Minimalist. https://www.becomingminimalist.com/more-generosity/

Beers, B. (2021, February 19). *Should I Pay off Debt or Invest Extra Cash?* Investopedia. https://www.investopedia.com/articles/pf/08/invest-reduce-debt.asp

Birken, E. G. (2020, March 5). *How To Budget In 7 Simple Steps*. Forbes Advisor. https://www.forbes.com/advisor/personal-finance/how-to-budget-simple-steps/

Borad, S. B. (2020, October 5). *Budgeting Process – Steps and Importance of Budget*. EFinanceManagement. https://efinancemanagement.com/budgeting/budgeting-process#:~:text=The%20budgeting%20process%20is%20the

Brennan, C. (2019, January 28). *Good Debt Vs. Bad Debt*. Forbes Advisor. https://www.forbes.com/advisor/loans/good-debt-vs-bad-debt/

Central Bank. (n.d.). *10 Strategies to Avoid Getting into Debt | Central Bank*. Www.centralbank.net. https://www.centralbank.net/learning-center/strategies-to-avoid-debt/

Chen, J. (2021, February 23). *Learn About Compounding*. Investopedia. https://www.investopedia.com/terms/c/compounding.asp

Compound Interest Calculator | Investor.gov. (n.d.). Www.investor.gov. https://www.investor.gov/financial-tools-calculators/calculators/compound-interest-calculator

Creating a Budget with a Personal Budget Spreadsheet. (2019). Better Money Habits. https://bettermoneyhabits.bankofamerica.com/en/saving-budgeting/creating-a-budget

Cruze, R. (2020a, September 25). *Impulse Buying: Why We Do It and How to Stop.* Daveramsey.com. https://www.daveramsey.com/blog/stop-impulse-buys#:~:text=We%20impulse%20buy%20because%20of

Cruze, R. (2020b, October 21). *How to Change Your Money Mindset.* Daveramsey.com. https://www.daveramsey.com/blog/understanding-your-money-mindset

Daly, L. (2019, November 24). *The 8 Biggest Benefits of Being Generous.* The Ascent. https://www.fool.com/the-ascent/banks/articles/8-biggest-benefits-being-generous/

Davis, G. B. (2021, March 1). *How to make a budget - 5 Steps to get started.* Money Crashers. https://www.moneycrashers.com/how-to-make-a-budget/

English rainy-day phrases explained by Susie Dent. (2018, September 21). *BBC News.* https://www.bbc.com/news/uk-england-42719824

Epperson, S., & Dickler, J. (2020, January 27). *The secret to financial success: Paying off debt.* CNBC. https://www.cnbc.com/2020/01/27/how-to-pay-off-debt.html

Evans, J. (2020, September 10). *Should I Pay Off Debt or Save Money?* Credit Counselling Society. https://nomoredebts.org/blog/dealing-with-debt/should-i-pay-off-debt-or-save-money#:~:text=Paying%20Off%20Debt%20Can%20Improve%20Your%20Credit%20Score&text=However%2C%20by%20paying%20down%20your

Farrington, R. (2018, January 29). *What Type Of Financial Expert Should You Hire For You?* The College Investor. https://thecollegeinvestor.com/21262/type-financial-expert-hire-situation/

Fernando, J. (2019). *Compound Interest Definition.* Investopedia. https://www.investopedia.com/terms/c/compoundinterest.asp

Fine Print: Should you read it or skip it? (n.d.). Www.araglegal.com. https://www.araglegal.com/individuals/learning-center/topics/budget-and-finance/when-fine-print-must-read

Five simple tips help you avoid impulse buying - The Chin Family. (n.d.). Www.ifec.org.hk. https://www.ifec.org.hk/web/en/young-adults/money-management/five-simple-tips-help-you-avoid-impulse-buying.page

Fonville, M. (2020, February 2). *9 Reasons Why Retirement Planning is Important.* Covenant. https://www.covenantwealthadvisors.com/post/9-reasons-why-retirement-planning-is-important

Gailey, A. (2020, July 7). *10 Money Experts You Should Be Following Right Now.* Time. https://time.com/nextadvisor/banking/personal-finance-experts-to-follow/

Generosity | SkillsYouNeed. (n.d.). Www.skillsyouneed.com. https://www.skillsyouneed.com/ps/generosity.html

George, D. (2020, May 11). *3 Reasons Why You Should Read the Small Print.* The Motley Fool. https://www.fool.com/the-ascent/banks/articles/reasons-why-you-should-read-small-print/

Government of Canada, F. C. A. of C. (2012, May 11). *Credit Card Payment Calculator.* Itools-Ioutils.fcac-Acfc.gc.ca. https://itools-ioutils.fcac-acfc.gc.ca/CCPC-CPCC/CCPCCalc-CPCCCalc-eng.aspx

Hall, L. (2018, August 8). *Keeping up with the Joneses is bad for your finances.* Www.morningstar.com.au. https://www.morningstar.com.au/learn/article/keeping-up-with-the-joneses-is-bad-for-your-f/169437#:~:text=Trying%20to%20%22keep%20up%20with

Hedreen, S. (2020, December 28). *How to Read the Fine Print of a Loan Agreement.* Business.com. https://www.business.com/articles/do-understand-the-fine-print-of-your-loan-agreement/

Hickey, J. P. (2015, July 3). *7 Reasons why generous people are successful.* Lifehack. https://www.lifehack.org/289468/7-reasons-generous-people-are-more-likely-successful

Hund, L. (2020, December 7). *Should You Pay Debt Before Saving?* Bankrate. https://www.bankrate.com/banking/savings/these-guidelines-will-help-you-decide-whether-to-pay-down-debt-or-save/

Irby, L. (2020a, February 4). *10 Strategies for Paying Off Your Debt When You're Broke.* The Balance. https://www.thebalance.com/how-to-pay-off-debt-when-you-re-broke-3875583

Irby, L. (2020b, October 31). *9 Reasons to Pay Off Your Debt.* The Balance. https://www.thebalance.com/reasons-to-pay-off-debt-960047

Is Keeping Up With The Joneses Keeping You Broke? (2019, September 1). The Investors Way. https://theinvestorsway.com.au/keeping-up-with-the-joneses/

Keeping Up With The Joneses: The Bad Habit That Costs You. (2020, March 15). Invested Wallet. https://investedwallet.com/keeping-up-with-the-joneses/

Keinath, S. (2018, December 26). *Understanding the basics of a budget.* 4-H Youth Money Management. https://www.canr.msu.edu/news/understanding-the-basics-of-a-budget

Kenton, W. (2020, December 30). *Fine Print.* Investopedia. https://www.investopedia.com/terms/f/fineprint.asp

Kline, B. (2017, May 17). *The Truth About Keeping up with the Joneses.* Thesavvycouple.com. https://thesavvycouple.com/truth-keeping-up-with-the-joneses/

Lee, D. (2016, January 10). *The Psychological Perks of Paying off Debt.* Bankrate.com. https://www.foxbusiness.com/features/the-psychological-perks-of-paying-off-debt

Leonhardt, M. (2020, February 13). *32% of American workers have medical debt—and over half have defaulted on it.* CNBC.

https://www.cnbc.com/2020/02/13/one-third-of-american-workers-have-medical-debt-and-most-default.html

Livingston, A. (n.d.). *17 Reasons Why You Should Get Out of Debt - Benefits of Being Debt-Free.* https://www.moneycrashers.com/reasons-get-out-debt/

Luenendonk, M. (2018, February 20). *Budgeting Process: Complete Guide.* Cleverism. https://www.cleverism.com/budgeting-process-complete-guide/

Lusinski, N. (2018, August 26). *11 financial experts share the best money advice they've ever received.* Business Insider. https://www.businessinsider.com/financial-experts-best-money-advice-2018-8

McMaken, L. (2019). *4 Types Of Insurance Everyone Needs.* Investopedia. https://www.investopedia.com/financial-edge/0212/4-types-of-insurance-everyone-needs.aspx

Menton, J. (2020, September 18). *"This IS Going to Bankrupt me": Americans Rack up $45B Worth of Medical Debt in Collections.* USA TODAY. https://www.usatoday.com/story/money/2020/09/18/unemployment-americans-face-45-b-worth-medical-debt-collections/3480192001/

O'Shea, B., & Schwahn, L. (2021, January 13). *Budgeting 101: How to Budget Money.* NerdWallet. https://www.nerdwallet.com/article/finance/how-to-budget

Rainy Day Fund or Emergency Fund. (2017, March 1). QuickBooks Canada. https://quickbooks.intuit.com/ca/resources/cash-flow/rainy-day-fund-emergency-fund/

Ramsey, D. (2018). *Tithes and Offerings.* Daveramsey.com. https://www.daveramsey.com/blog/daves-advice-on-tithing-and-giving

Ramsey, D. (2021, February 23). *25 Ways to Get Out of Debt.* Daveramsey.com. https://www.daveramsey.com/blog/ways-to-get-out-of-debt

Retirement Planning - Importance of Retirement Planning | ICICI Prulife. (n.d.). Www.iciciprulife.com. https://www.iciciprulife.com/retirement-pension-plans/retirement-planning.html

Rieck, D. (2010, March 3). *Give and Grow Rich: The Power of Focused Generosity.* Copyblogger. https://copyblogger.com/give-and-grow-rich/

Rogin, E. (2019, June 17). *Can Generosity Make You Wealthier?* https://www.ellenrogin.com/generosity-benefits-health-wealth-happiness/

Save for a Rainy Day. (n.d.). https://foh.psc.gov/whatwedo/eap/S-F30E-FOH%20Financial%20Future%20Source.pdf

Save something for a rainy day Idiom Definition – Grammarist. (n.d.). Grammarist.com. Retrieved March 8, 2021, from https://grammarist.com/idiom/save-something-for-a-rainy-day/#:~:text=To%20save%20something%20for%20a%20rainy%20day%20means%20to%20set

Scotia Bank. (n.d.). *Importance of Planning for Retirement.* Www.scotiabank.com. https://www.scotiabank.com/ca/en/personal/investing/investing-basics/importance-of-planning-retirement.html#:~:text=Personal%20planning%20is%20important%20because

Shinn, L. (2021, January 25). *Rule of Thumb: Should I Pay Off Debt or Invest for Retirement?* The Balance. https://www.thebalance.com/should-you-pay-off-your-debt-or-invest-356371

Should I Pay Down Debt or Focus on Savings? | Equifax. (n.d.). Www.equifax.com. Retrieved March 8, 2021, from https://www.equifax.com/personal/education/covid-19/debt-repayment-vs-saving-money/

Should you save, or pay off loans and cards? (n.d.). Www.moneyadviceservice.org.uk. Retrieved March 8, 2021, from https://www.moneyadviceservice.org.uk/en/articles/should-i-save-or-pay-off-debt

Sivens, N. S. (2020, March 16). *The 8 Types Of Financial Experts And How They Can Help You*. Girlboss. https://www.girlboss.com/read/financial-advisors

Six Tips on How to Avoid Debt | New York Life. (n.d.). Www.newyorklife.com. https://www.newyorklife.com/articles/avoid-being-young-and-in-debt

Smith, L. (2019). *Good Debt vs. Bad Debt: What's the Difference?* Investopedia. https://www.investopedia.com/articles/pf/12/good-debt-bad-debt.asp

Staff, I. (2020, December 29). *Saving vs. Paying off Debt*. Investopedia. https://www.investopedia.com/financial-edge/0212/saving-vs.-paying-off-debt.aspx

The Australian Parenting Website. (n.d.). *Managing money and avoiding debt*. Raising Children Network. https://raisingchildren.net.au/grown-ups/family-life/managing-money/money-debt

Three reasons why you should pay off debt and invest at the same time. | New York Life. (n.d.). Www.newyorklife.com. https://www.newyorklife.com/articles/3-reasons-why-pay-off-debt-and-invest-at-the-same-time

Vessella, V. (n.d.). *There's Some Cool Psychology Behind Impulse Buys [Infographic]*. Www.repsly.com. https://www.repsly.com/blog/consumer-goods/theres-some-cool-psychology-behind-impulse-buys-infographic

Vohwinkle, J. (2019). *Your 6-Step Guide to Making a Personal Budget*. The Balance. https://www.thebalance.com/how-to-make-a-budget-1289587

Vohwinkle, J. (2020, May 17). *Why Do I Need Insurance?* The Balance. https://www.thebalance.com/insurance-basics-why-do-i-need-insurance-1289684#:~:text=You%20need%20insurance%20to%20protect

What is Budgeting and Why is it Important? | My Money Coach. (2000). Mymoneycoach.ca.

https://www.mymoneycoach.ca/budgeting/what-is-a-budget-planning-forecasting

What is Impulsive Buying? Definition of Impulsive Buying, Impulsive Buying Meaning - The Economic Times. (2019). The Economic Times. https://economictimes.indiatimes.com/definition/impulsive-buying

What Is Insurance And Why Is It So Important? (2020, June 26). Www.etmoney.com. https://www.etmoney.com/blog/know-everything-about-insurance-and-why-you-should-have-insurance/

What is retirement planning? Why is it important? (2020, September 8). Scripbox. https://scripbox.com/mf/retirement-planning/

What Psychology Knows about Impulse Buying in 2020. (n.d.). Www.newneuromarketing.com. https://www.newneuromarketing.com/what-psychology-knows-about-impulse-buying-in-2020

Why do I need insurance? (n.d.). Great Eastern, Brunei. https://www.greateasternlife.com/bn/en/personal-insurance/understand-insurance/why-do-i-need-insurance.html

Why do you need insurance? (2019). Cooperators.ca. https://www.cooperators.ca/en/Resources/protect-what-matters/why-do-you-need-insurance.aspx

Yeager, J. (n.d.). *12 Ways to Avoid Impulse Buying and Save Money - Buyers Remorse, Shopping.* AARP. https://www.aarp.org/money/budgeting-saving/info-10-2010/savings_challenge_tips_for_impulse_shopping.html

Zimmerman, I. (2012). *What Motivates Impulse Buying?* Psychology Today. https://www.psychologytoday.com/us/blog/sold/201207/what-motivates-impulse-buying

Investing For Beginners

*How to Save, Invest and Grow
Your Wealth Through the Stock
Market, Real Estate, Index
Funds, Precious Metals, and
More*

Joel Jacobs

Introduction

Does one need to be a financial expert to trade and invest? Absolutely not. One needs to learn the basics of the financial market and then learn what works for them and what does not. Are you someone who wants short-term investments with huge risks but even higher payouts? Or are you someone who would rather make long-term investments to retire comfortably? Would you rather actively have control over your assets or have a professional handle them at a cost? Investing has a lot of subsets and strategies that can be molded to suit the individual.

Investments do incur risks; however, those risks can be minimized with the right trading tools and proper help. Investors know that they will incur losses, which is why they ensure that their generated revenues surpass those losses. Making smart financial investments can be profitable both in the short and the long run. There is no perfect time to start investing, so anyone interested in investing can begin trading anytime. Financial securities like stocks and shares have many variations that can benefit anyone depending on their financial standing and investment goals. Also, stocks and shares are not the only options when it comes to investing in the market. There are bonds, mutual funds, precious metals, and even real estate that one could invest in to generate revenues. In addition, many trading strategies exist for each of the financial securities, meaning there is an investment option for everyone.

So, want to tap into the world of investing but have no idea where to start? It might sound obvious, but in order to fully comprehend how investments work, we need to start at the very beginning and give definitions to all the terms that are going to be used persistently in this book. Learning the basics allows for a better understanding of the more complex notions of investing. It permits you, a future investor, to be fully comfortable with every aspect of the trade.

Chapter 1: Investment Basics for Beginners

What Is the Stock Market?

The stock market is a cluster of exchanges and markets that participate in the buying, selling, and trading of public and private company investment securities. Investment securities are tradable financials such as stocks, equities, and debt used to raise capital in both public and private markets with the purpose of retaining them for investment. These shares are almost always from public companies because private companies do not exchange their shares on the public stock market. Keep in mind that while private companies are not publicly traded, they still have shares that are kept and traded internally for their selective group of shareholders, such as employees. Let us return to the stock market. A country can have multiple stock exchange venues that follow the same regulations set in place by formal business institutions. In everyday dialogue, the terms stock market and stock exchange are often used interchangeably. However, a stock market is a collection of stock exchanges. For clarification, any market participating in the exchange of stocks and other financial securities is considered a stock market. In comparison, a stock exchange is the place where such trades are happening. For example, someone claiming they trade on the stock market means that they participate in purchasing and selling shares through one or more stock exchanges that the stock market encompasses. Some of the most popular American stock exchanges include NASDAQ and the New York Stock Exchange, which make up part of the American stock market.

To fully understand the purpose of the stock market, imagine that you are window shopping for a pair of jeans. Thankfully, the area that you live in is packed with denim vendors eager for your money. They will compete with each other to offer their consumers the best price for their product. Because of this, you are offered a fair price and are able to peruse the options before making your choice.

However, your friend Ben lives in a smaller town with only one denim vendor and is forced to purchase from that one vendor when he needs jeans. Similarly, the stock market is the meeting place of various options when it comes to shares and stocks. This abundance of financial securities ensures fair pricing, healthy competition, and trading security in a secure and controlled environment. With the use of modern-day technology, the stock market operates electronically, allowing for zero to low operational risk.

There are various markets within the stock market that have different specializing characteristics, despite an occasional overlap in functionality. Two subcategories of stock markets include the equity market and the share market.

What Is the Equity Market?

As part of the stock market, the equity market refers to the buying and selling of ownership shares of public companies through the stock exchange. Therefore, the equity market does not deal with the exchanging of privately traded stocks. Both terms are synonymous in investing because purchasing a share of stock constitutes an equity interest in a company. Someone buying a stake in a company has the expectation to benefit from their investment, either through the price of the stock increasing or receiving a share of the profits. Just like stock markets, equity markets are an all-encompassing term for all global stock exchanges that pair public stock buyers with public stock sellers. The biggest examples of equity markets include the New York Stock Exchange, Hong Kong Exchanges, and Euronet Europe. The equity market is typically the stock market that people are the most familiar with, and at its core, it follows a free-market economic system. Public companies turn a profit by participating in the equity market and allowing investors to purchase ownership of the said company through shares. The number of shares an investor possesses determines the percentage of company ownership they have.

However, while the stock market deals with both public and private company stocks, the equity market focuses on public company stocks. Stocks are offered by buyers at prices and then sellers will bid for their specific prices, and when the two match, a sale happens. The price of an asset in the marketplace or its value determined by the investment community is referred to as the market value. This is easy to determine for exchange-traded securities like stocks. These stocks are considered liquid since they are easily bought, sold and traded, which influences their market value. For example, if there are a high number of investments in a company then the price of their stock will rise. On the other hand, an increase in investors selling their stocks of a company will decrease the value of their stocks.

What Is the Share Market?

As previously discussed, the share market is a subset of the stock market that handles the purchasing and selling of shares, which represent a unit of ownership of whichever company the share comes from. The purchasing of shares permits companies to maintain their upkeep and allows investors to trade shares to profit. Since the exchange of shares also happens in an equity market, it is easy to confuse the two markets and their similarities. A difference between the two is that a shareholder, or someone investing in company shares, owns the shares of one specific company. In contrast, an equity stockholder is someone who buys stock in any company. Both are very similar but found in different categories of the stock market.

What Is the Over-the-Counter Market?

Independent stock exchanges are called over-the-counter (OTC) markets, and just like their physical stock exchange counterparts, they exist all over the globe. These are decentralized markets in which the participants can directly trade stocks, currencies, and more without the need for a broker. They do not have a physical location; instead, all exchanges are performed electronically or over the phone. These are very different from auction-based market systems, where buyers and sellers both simultaneously compete in bidding and offering of stocks. The price of an exchanged stock through this system represents the lowest rate a seller is willing to sell and the highest rate a buyer is willing to spend. This kind of market has two types of clientele: a broker trading with their clients, including corporations and institutions, is called a "customer market," while two traders exchanging with each other are referred to as an "interdealer" market.

In over-the-counter markets, however, dealers participate in shaping the market by creating their own prices to buy and sell a security or another financial product. Due to there being fewer regulations in OTC markets than physical stock markets, exchanges can occur without anyone else knowing much about the trade, including the pricing of the transaction. Because of this, over-the-counter markets are less transparent and have liquidity due to the occasional lack of both buyers and sellers. The dependency on the market influencing dealers can make it troublesome to buy and sell stocks in the future.

What Are Primary and Secondary Markets?

Markets fall into one of two divisions: primary and secondary markets. In the primary market is the creation of new financial securities, including bills and stocks for companies trading for the first time, usually at a pre-determined or arranged price. This market issues and sells new stocks and bonds to the public. A popular example of such is an initial public offering or IPO. During an initial public offering, a business transpires between the purchasing investor and the financing bank in charge of underwriting the IPO. An important thing to understand is that securities created by the primary market are purchased straight from an issuer. Governments and companies will both use this market by issuing new securities in order to expand business operations and to cover research and development expenses. They achieve this because the majority of the funding earned goes to the issuer of the securities-in this case, the companies and governments. Financing that does not go to an issuer can go to an investment bank that intervenes and regulates the initial pricing of securities, receiving a portion of the funding for facilitating sales. Trading on the primary market is also beneficial for investors who will commonly pay less on securities compared to the secondary market.

While the primary market handles stocks when they are first issued to the public, the secondary market encompasses the purchasing and selling of securities that investors already own. In this way, investors trade with each other instead of trading with the financial security issuing entity. Since there are many independent but interconnected trades, the secondary market acts as an equalizer, driving the price of securities towards their actual valued price. When most people think of investing and the stock market, they are thinking of the secondary market. The most commonly traded securities in the secondary market are stocks; however, they are definitely not the only financial asset traded on this market. Individual investors, corporations, and investment banks can purchase and trade bonds and mutual funds, such as real estate mortgages, on the secondary market. All these trades benefit the selling investor who receives all the proceeds from their sales instead of the company issuing the stock or the bank underwriting the IPO.

Secondary market transactions are called this because they are one step removed from the original securities created in the primary market. For instance, a financial institution creating mortgage security by writing mortgages for consumers would be the primary market. Then, the bank would sell such securities to real estate corporations and associations on the secondary market.

Who Are Brokers?

Brokers are firms or individuals who act as intermediaries between investors and the exchange of securities. They are essential because securities exchanges only approve of orders and trades between individuals and firms already participating in that exchange. Therefore, individual investors and traders require the services of exchange members, or brokers. These financial intermediaries are compensated for their service through administrative fees, commissions, or getting paid directly from the trade itself. Brokers can also provide potential investors with financial guidance by offering their market intelligence, investment plans, and client-tailored market research.

In investing, there are two types of brokers: discount brokers and full-service brokers. The former administers exchanges on their client's behalf without typically providing financial advice or insight. At the same time, the latter includes tailored financial investment solutions and advice in addition to their exchange service. Due to the growth of online stock exchanges, the number of discount brokers has increased immensely. They are great for self-directed investors who do not require any investment advice or research services. Discount brokers are often paid in fees rather than a commission. They keep their prices cheap due to the volume of trading they execute and their lower administrative costs compared to brokers working on non-online platforms.

In comparison, full-service brokers offer a variety of services ranging from market research to retirement planning, in addition to their investment products. Because of all of this, these brokers charge potential investors far more in commission for their services. Full-service brokers are then compensated through a brokerage firm based on both trading volume and investment product sales. Recently, instead of a commission payment system, some full-service brokers offer investment products and services for a set fee; this can include products like managing clients' investment accounts.

Despite the terms "broker" and "trader" being used synonymously in everyday conversation, there is a notable distinction between the two. A trader is someone who trades and buys stocks on behalf of a portfolio manager, while a broker is a licensed financial sales agent. There are many similarities between the two, such as they both sell and trade securities for their clientele, who can either be individuals or corporations. However, the main difference is that the broker has direct contact with their clients while the trader does not.

What Is a Demat Account?

A dematerialized account, or Demat account for short, provides the convenience of maintaining financial securities in an electronic format. It holds all of an individual's investments, including shares, exchange-traded funds, and bonds, in one place. Thus, investors participating in online trading with a Demat account benefit from electronic security, convenience, and cost-effectiveness. Dematerialization in this sense is the process of converting traditional physical share certificates into electronic forms, offering a modernized, easy-to-maintain format for investors to see all their holdings at any time and anywhere in the world. Due to their online formatting, Demat accounts help reduce costs and risks associated with physical certificates, and paperwork. They also offer users the ease of seeing all their investments in one place quickly, without the need for a paper trail.

Think of Demat accounts like a bank account. Just like a bank account, a dematerialized account holds the account holder's securities in electronic form instead of a physical form and keeps track of credits and debits of their financial securities.

Why Do Shares Fluctuate?

The price of shares changes every day by market forces, following the concept of supply-demand economics. This means that if the demand for shares surpasses the supply of current shares, then the price increases to match the demand. This happens because many buyers want the same limited shares, therefore driving up the price as only those with the capital can purchase them. The opposite also applies; if the supply of shares surpasses the demand, the price will drop to entice people to buy the supply surplus. This is the reason for the daily fluctuations in shares. The supply and demand of shares globally are determined by individual corporations and how financially well they do. In addition, there are other external and internal variables that can fluctuate the pricing of shares, depending on their effect on the market. These price fluctuations are seen as market risk and are beyond the investors' control.

What Are Dividends?

Publicly-listed companies can reward investors who put money into their venture in the form of dividends. A dividend gets distributed out of a company's earnings to a select group of its shareholders, who are determined by the company's board of directors. These income distributions are typically cash, but they can also be in the form of additional stock in the company. Dividend payouts are commonly accompanied by a proportional increase in the company's stock price. Although dividends come out of a company's profits, they can still be paid out if profits are not made. The reason for this is to maintain a public image for current investors and potential new ones.

The board of directors can decide both the number of payout rates and the frequency of dividend payouts. Quarterly payouts are common; however, they can also be paid out monthly or yearly. Through scheduled or individual dividend payouts, companies might issue non-recurring special dividends for investors as a bonus reward. An example of such a special dividend is Microsoft, who, due to strong business performance and an increased financial outlook, issued a $3 per share in 2004 while the average at the time was $0.08 to $0.16 per share.

Dividends create a dialogue of trust between investors and companies, following the concept of "I scratch your back, you scratch mine." Companies will reward investors in hopes of more investments leading to future higher dividend payouts. These company payouts also offer insight into a companies' financial situation and can be a way to reassure shareholders about the future of the company. Companies with long, robust dividend payout records are often more trusted than the alternative. A reduction or complete elimination of a dividend payout could indicate to investors that the company is in trouble; it can also mean that the board of directors decided that the profits were better used for internal investment. Perhaps investing that financial surplus into a new product or service could triple profits in the future, and this was deemed as more important.

The best dividend payers are often larger, established companies in the market with predictable profits. They issue regular dividends to maximize shareholder wealth and build a rapport of trust with their investors. The companies often work in healthcare, the oil industry, banks, utilities, and basic materials. Start-ups and companies known for high growth, like the technology industry, may not offer dividends to their investors. These early-stage companies may incur high costs and losses that could have been used for the company. These companies might not have enough profit to supply dividends but still make enough money to sustain themselves. Companies might also not pay out dividends in order to invest their profits back into the business, especially during the process of expansion or moments of high growth.

What Types of Investors Are There?

In stock exchanges, there are two main types of investors: short-term and long-term investors. Short-term investors are traders who will buy and sell shares daily or weekly in order to profit on the face value price fluctuations of their shares. This kind of investor can also hold their shares for longer amounts of time but will commonly sell their shares when the price is high. At the same time, they buy shares when stock prices are lower than usual or when a market price increase is upcoming. On the other hand, long-term investors will buy stocks in bulk and invest over a long period of time. These types of investors do not worry about the face value growth of the shares. Instead, they are concerned with the dividend payouts from their company investments.

In more depth, short-term investors hold their financial securities for less than a year, typically for a couple of months, and use their liquidity and active trading strategies to generate revenues. These forms of investment include but are not limited to short-term bonds, stocks, ETFs, and more. Short-term investors count on the volatility of their investments. The fluctuations in price allow for these traders to profit off a financial asset in a certain amount of time. Despite the relatively small price movements of these assets in the market, these securities usually have high liquidity, ensuring that investors can sell them fairly quickly. Traders in this category can trade multiple securities with smaller price fluctuations to make smaller, more consistent gains. They can also act on the high volatility of certain assets and attempt to capitalize on sudden, more drastic price movements. An example of this is an investor selling their stocks after they have experienced appreciation in price, therefore earning in profits the difference between the sold price and the initial purchased price. Short-term investments are usually a form of active investing and carry a higher risk of losing capital since the market can fluctuate in any direction. One bad investing decision can cost traders a lot of money. Therefore, a lot of research, market knowledge, and confidence are needed to comfortably trade securities in the short term.

Long-term investors, on the other hand, hold the majority of their assets for up to a couple of years. These long-term investments are commonplace in financial portfolios with a specific investing strategy tailored for the investor. These investments include mutual funds, long-term savings accounts, and bonds. Although almost any investment can become a long-term one, securities with slow but steady value appreciations are favored. Illiquid investments, or securities that cannot be quickly transferred into cash, are also common long-term investments. Real estate is a popular long-term investment, where investors will buy properties and let them naturally appreciate in value. Other than this, long-term investments make for good college funds and retirement accounts because these portfolios count on long-term value growth and limited trading and transactions. These longer investments are considered a form of passive investing since less oversight and management is needed.

These two types contain many subsets and hybrids of the two investment ideologies, which can be tailored to individual financial circumstances and investment goals. This will be explored more in-depth in future chapters.

What Are Sectors?

Industries and sectors are synonymous terms that define any given economy in a market. Companies get assigned an industry based on their primary line of business, and their associations with similar industries are aggregated into a major sector. Therefore, sectors are huge generic categories of about a dozen economic industries , with each industry followed by sub-industries.

The majority of economies have four sectors, which in turn are cut into sub-sectors. The first of these sectors is the primary sector, which consists of the extraction of earth's natural products. Industries in this sector are agriculture, mining, and forestry. The secondary sector involves manufacturing and the processing of the primary sector's products into new goods. The tertiary sector provides services for products such as entertainment firms, retailers, and financial institutions. The last sector, titled the quaternary sector, includes companies working with intellectual pursuits, such as educational organizations.

Sectors allow investors to invest their money in classified business industries such as healthcare, technology, and telecommunications. Each and every sector has its own characteristics and associated risks that attract investors. Because of this, many economic analysts will specialize in one sector, with large companies having many advisors per sector. This also creates the notion of sector investing, where one may only invest in one sector they deem beneficial for them. The gas and oil industry is a popular sector that attracts many specialized investments. Stocks will often trend alongside their respective sector, meaning if a whole sector is having a rough year, chances are any stocks associated with that sector will fall. Therefore, having an understanding of the market will allow investors to estimate the rise and fall of a particular stock from whichever sector, based on the sector's overall performance.

Chapter 2: Investment in Stocks and Options

Now with the basics of investing and financial securities defined, we are ready to delve into the actual art of investing in stocks and options. First, we must categorize the different types of trading that can occur before further explaining the various forms of stocks and options in the financial investment world. These trading strategies all have their pros and cons. Each investor needs to determine which strategy works for them based on their initial capital and investment goals.

As a refresher, stocks are tiny portions of a public company that anyone can buy, or in the case of private companies, only internal shareholders can buy. An investor buying a stock in a company is investing money into a company and hoping that that stock will increase in value in the future, which is based on the company's financial well-being in question. Since the prices of stocks change daily, they are considered volatile. Thus, it is smart to buy stocks in different industries to have a diverse investment portfolio. A diverse portfolio will ensure that the investor has other investments to bounce back on even if one sector falls. Stocks are purchased either at physical locations such as an auction-based stock exchange like the New York Stock Exchange or through an online platform like NASDAQ.

The benefits of trading in stocks long-term are dividends, those regular company payouts to shareholders which depend on the company's current financial situation. For long-term stock investors, picking a larger company with a history of high regular dividend payouts and limited debt is key. Despite short-term stock traders forgoing dividends, they can still profit by buying stocks at low prices and selling them when their value increases. Since stocks fluctuate daily, this can be a quick way to make money.

As aforementioned, stock prices fluctuate easily, and their volatile nature can make them a risky investment. While one stock buyer is hoping that their purchased stocks will increase in value, another stock seller is anticipating for them to crash. With these changes happening so quickly, it can be difficult to know when to buy and sell. It is all about finding the investment technique that works for you based on your characteristics. Stock trading is fast and requires lots of time spent watching the market; however, it allows for quick profit if done right. The rapid pace of trading is also why a diverse financial portfolio is key when participating in the stock exchange. Investing in different sectors and having various kinds of investments spreads out the possibility of risk and allows you to maximize profit. Never put all your eggs in one basket.

Strategies of Trading in Stocks and Options

There are different styles of trading depending on the investor's goals and how quickly the investor can make a profit. There are long-term and short-term styles that can be used in conjunction with each other while other strategies oppose each other. It all depends on the investor's trading style and their aspired investment goals. All forms of trading can be categorized into two styles of investing: active and passive.

Active investing is a hands-on approach that requires someone to act as portfolio manager, whether they are hired or the investor themself. The goal of active investing is to take advantage of short-term price fluctuations to beat the stock market's average returns. This requires a deeper understanding of the market and the variables that affect the value of all securities. Most portfolio managers have a team of employees who use both quantitative and qualitative factors to make educated assumptions of market price changes to know when to buy and sell shares. This requires not only a vast knowledge of investing but also confidence in those trading decisions. A good portfolio manager must be more right than wrong about price fluctuations and good investments.

Passive investing is a long-term style of investing and is more cost-effective since the number of trades and transactions is limited. Passive investors cannot get swayed by market sentiment, fluctuations, and the temptation to anticipate the market's next move. This style of investing requires a buy-and-hold mentality just to allow the securities to run their course in order to benefit in the long term. Index Funds are good examples of passive investment as they are many tiny pieces of shares that participate in the overall uptrend of the market. This way, investors earn their returns over a long time, keeping their eye on the prize ahead and not caving into short-term shortcomings and setbacks.

A combination of both styles for short-term and long-term returns is favorable for any investor. Using a passive investment like a Mutual Fund to secure retirement income while actively day-trading shares for bigger short-term returns is an example of this.

Trend Trading

Trend Trading is a style of trading that involves following the market trends of industries and stocks to make investments. When the price of a stock fluctuates upwards or downwards, that is referred to as a trend. Trend trading analyzes the market for trends and uses that to take advantage of either uptrends or downtrends. Stocks that are on an uptrend mean that their value increases, with higher swing lows and higher swing highs. In contrast, value decreasing stocks on a downtrend experience lower swing highs and lower swing lows. Swing lows are when the lows of stock are lower than the surrounding stock prices at any given time. Swing highs are the opposite of a swing low, meaning the stock price is higher than other high stocks in that given time. Swing highs are usually the peak of a stock's value and are followed by a decline. This form of trading is great for investing beginners due to the ease of its application.

Investors who are trend trading will use these market trends to enter either a long position or a short position. Joining a long position refers to when an investor buys stocks with the assumption that they will rise in value in order to sell them at a profit in the future. This strategy is considered a long-term investment as one must wait for that uptrend. Historically, the stock market usually appreciates over time; however, that does not mean that those assumptions are always right and that a market crash is impossible. A global pandemic, anyone?

The opposite of a long position is a short position, which is when an investor sells their stock at its current price with the intention to rebuy it at a lower price after a downtrend. Short position trend trading is shorter term but riskier since there is more room for failure than there is for success. This is because investors in this position rely on a stock decreasing and their profits are based on how close to zero the value of the stock is. As mentioned before, the stock market is more likely to appreciate in value rather than depreciate. In short position trading, there are two types of short positioning: naked short and covered short. The former involves trading stocks that one does not own, while the latter borrows shares through a stock loan department to sell.

Naked shorting is a controversial topic since it is illegal in the United States, despite it still happening through regulation loopholes. Naked shorting is the act of short-selling shares that one does not own or have not been proven to exist. This has an impact on the liquidity of financial security in the marketplace. It allows investors to participate in a non-available stock exchange. If other investors also take part, it increases the liquidity and demand of a share that investors cannot obtain.

Contrarian Trading

Contrarian Trading is an eponymous investment style that involves investors intentionally going against market trends by selling stocks when most are buying and vice versa to turn profits. These types of investors argue that investors who follow trends are often too late for the market movement to be beneficial. Meaning, if the majority of people are assuming that the market will continue to uptrend, then the market is most likely already at its peak. The same works in reverse-if a downturn is predicted, that means the shares have already sold out and that the market can only start going upwards from here. Contrarian trading is built around the notion of market herd mentality that can fluctuate the market trends. While most people are following trends, contrarian investors are using other investors' pessimism to buy stocks that are deemed invaluable or sell stocks that everyone is buying in hopes of an uptrend.

This way of investing is more long-term because most of these investors buy undervalued stocks with the intention to sell once the value rebounds. This strategy does lead to profits when those undervalued stocks start to rise; however, it is a possibility that the stock will never recover. Because they do not follow trends, these investors can miss out big when the market trends are correct.

Candlestick Trading

Candlestick charts are used to show the link between price and the supply-demand influenced by the emotion of traders. Having originated from Japan in the 1700s when analyzing the rice market, candlestick charts use different colors to represent the size of price moves. Different colors are used to show which emotion is being displayed and its impact on price movements. These charts help traders determine possible price fluctuations based on past market patterns. A daily candlestick chart shows the four price points, which are open, close, high, and low.

Price Action Trading

Price Action Trading involves reading the current market based on historical data and price movements to make a subjective decision of whether or not to buy, sell or trade securities. Traders of this style will use technical analysis tools such as trend lines, financial charts, and high/low swings to create their unique strategy for trading. This requires an in-depth understanding of the market and comfort with data analytics.

Since this form of trading is based on the investor's subjectivity, no two traders will react the same way to price fluctuations, with one buying securities when another would sell. These subjective decisions are assisted by market research and data, but every trader has their own price point limitations, behavioral patterns, and interpretations of the market. One trader might use an upward trend, enter a long position and buy securities on the assumption that the security will continue to increase. Another can interpret an upward trend with an upcoming decline, enter a short position, and sell their securities while the price value is high.

The market can be unpredictable, and there is no sure-fire way to guess the future of price value. Price action trading is good for short- to medium-term investments and profit trades rather than long-term investments. Traders must use subjective thinking and data analytic tools to identify potentially profitable trade opportunities. It also has a lot of support in the investing industry.

Price action trading offers flexibility and independence to traders who understand the market and have access to market data. In addition to the ease of exchanging securities through trading software, this trading style allows investors to feel like they are in control of their investments and make the decisions that could make or break their investment portfolio.

News Trading

As aforementioned, the stock market usually trends upwards; however, crashes and other downfalls can destroy an investor's financial portfolio. Therefore, trading news about the market should be an integral part of any investor. A day trader should stay abreast of trading news and do so multiple times during an exchange session, while long-term investors need to follow trade news less frequently.

Most market trading news is scheduled, and these include quarterly economic reports and corporations' economic updates. These news updates can positively affect one sector while negatively affecting another, which is another reason why it is imperative to diversify one's portfolio to cushion one's losses with other securities. However, trading news does foster a herd investment mentality. Therefore if an investor is subjectively confident in their investment securities, they will stick to them. It is very contrarian, however, it has been stated that the market crowd sentiment is not always right.

Trading news is classified into two categories: recurring and one-time. Recurring news is scheduled news releases that fluctuate the market, and these refer to business' quarterly earning reports, bank interest rate announcements, and economic data releases. One-time news is unexpected events that affect the market; usually, these events are more bad than good. These events can include but are not limited to terrorist attacks, pandemics, and bankruptcy from corporations and countries. Market news can affect a specific stock, an industry or sector, or the whole market.

As an investor, trading news is a must in order to know when, where, and which sector to invest in. Keeping in mind important dates for corporations that you participate in is important to track fluctuations in the market. Have a strategy both for good trading news and bad; always know your exit route in case of investing emergencies. Avoid rash decisions by seeing the big picture of the market. An immediate fall in the agriculture industry due to a faulty tractor contract might mean new lower swing lows that could see an uptrend in the future. Every investor has their own maximum risk levels; what is yours? It is easy to get swayed by the market crowd sentiment. However, sometimes investors must know when to use the news to their advantage and when to ignore it. Investors in long-term positions have more freedom in ignoring news that will not affect their long position investments. The bottom line is that trading news is paramount in upkeeping one's portfolio and taking advantage of the market to boost investments and profits.

Algorithm Trading

Algorithm Trading, or automatic trading, uses online investment software that follows a determined set of rules or an algorithm to accomplish the trade of securities. The algorithm will perform trades based on rules set by the investor that include time, price, quantity, or anything else that can be input mathematically. This form of trading can generate a larger number of trades and at a greater speed than a human investor. It also makes trading more systematic by removing the market impact of human emotion from the equation as well as rendering the market more liquid.

Using a computer program to facilitate trades eliminates the need for the investor to manually keep track of market fluctuations and live security pricing. The algorithm set in place by the investor will automatically buy and sell securities whenever the trader's criteria are met. Trades through this system are executed instantly at the best selling price through the investment software and are timed to avoid changes in pricing. This automated investment strategy reduces manual human error and removes emotional trading that can be costly. Historical financial data and real-time data through the software can also help to validate trading strategies.

Traders also use automatic trading in different investment strategies to generate profits. Adopting market trends is a popular way to invest through this system. Using historical data to view trends, one can set up an algorithm to buy and sell when the securities are at their respective highs and lows. Also, since trades on this software are instant, investors use this platform to purchase low-priced securities in one market to resell them simultaneously in another market for a higher price. These almost risk-free profitable trades are called arbitrage opportunities and just require an implemented algorithm to notice the use of price differentials to place orders.

Fundamental Trading

Fundamental trading refers to a strategy where traders will focus on market or company-specific events to determine when to buy stocks and who to buy them from. This method is associated with long-term buy-and-hold strategies rather than short-term daily traders. Buy-and-hold refers to buying stocks and holding onto them regardless of market fluctuations in the hopes of a substantially profitable long-term return.

Fundamentalists make their trades based on fundamentalist analysis, which includes corporation economic releases. These releases are anticipated, actual or historical financial reports, company acquisitions, and reorganizations in addition to stock splits. These traders use this quantitative data to search for investment opportunities; however, with millions of people also investing, it can be hard to acquire any information or data that someone else does not already have. Despite this, there is a usual boost in trades after these earning reports, creating a short-term investing opportunity.

Stock Splits are also important in fundamental trading. For example, a company takes their $40 stock and splits it 2 for 1. There is now double the number of stocks on the market selling for $20. This stock split doesn't change the company's capital on the market, but more people are willing to buy a $20 stock compared to a $40 stock. Using stock splits and historical data, an investor can identify the four phases of stock split appreciation and depreciation. In the pre-split, the value of the stock will typically increase while decreasing in the post-split. Using this information, short-term split stock traders can generate profit multiple times in one day with the same stock.

Another part of fundamentalist analysis is acquisitions and corporate takeovers. These acquisitions follow the same market trend as stock splits. Oftentimes they have an uptrend during the takeover speculation phase of the acquisition announcement followed by an immediate downtrend afterward. Fundamentalist traders use these trends, historical data, and investment analysis to make subjective, fair decisions when it comes to trading.

Sentimental Trading

Sentimental trading is the act of trading securities based on the sentiment of the overall market and could be classified as the opposite of contrarian trading. The market sentiment is the majority consensus to the overall state of a stock or the market. Two terms come into play when referring to sentiments of the market: bullish and bearish. A bullish investor or a bull is one who believes that security prices will go up. This term can also describe the market as a whole; if the market sentiment is that prices will increase, then the market sentiment is bullish. Bearish is the contrary sentiment, meaning that a bearish investor or bear will think prices are falling.

These investor sentiments are not always based on fundamental analysis. Instead, they are driven by human emotion. Day traders and other financial analysts will use the market sentiment because short-term price movements are often influenced by investor attitudes towards particular financial security or industry. Contrarian investors also use market sentiment in order to trade in the opposing direction of the market. These attitudes can cause securities to be over- or undervalued in the market. This is why there are indicators used to measure market sentiment to gather more quantitative data. However, the majority of sentimental trading is based on the overall consensus of investors towards the market.

Pattern Trading

This style of trading involves using price patterns which are price movements that are tracked using curves and trendlines. This allows investors to recognize falling and rising trends in the market, which helps influence their trades. These patterns are noticeable formations created by connecting different price points such as opening and closing prices with a line on a graph. By using these formations, technical and financial analysts identify patterns to anticipate the future price movements of securities.

Trendlines are lines connecting the various highs and lows of price points during a time period. If a trendline is curved upwards, referred to as an up trendline, this means prices of a security are experiencing new higher peaks and new higher troughs or lows. In contrast, a down trendline signifies prices are experiencing lower troughs and lower highs. Trendlines with more than two price points are generally more sustainable and better for making informed investment decisions.

Swing Trading

Swing trading attempts to capture short to medium-term gains in securities for a profit over the span of days or weeks. Swing traders will use fundamental and technical analysis in conjunction with price trends and patterns for finding investment opportunities. The goal of this strategy is to catch capital gain on price movements by identifying an asset's next move, entering a position, and then profiting if that price change happens. The most popular financial security to trade in swing trading is large-cap stocks. Stocks swing between broad defined highs and lows over the course of days and weeks. Swing investors will follow these waves and reverse when the stocks do, keeping up with the value.

This form of trading is one of the most popular for short to medium-term opportunities. Some swing investors will choose volatile stocks with lots of movement to speed up the daily process. At the same time, others go for more sedated stocks which might take longer to profit from but also limits risk. Both these investors, however, are open to running the risk of opening a session after a night or a weekend to substantially different prices. Abrupt market fluctuations such as one-time news announcements can also result in substantial losses. Due to the short-term nature of swing trading, these investors often miss out on longer-term trends and opportunities in favor of quicker financial gain.

The major difference between swing trading and day trading is the length of time involved. Day traders will close out their position at the end of the day when the market closes. However, swing traders will often hold onto securities overnight, risking gaps up and down against the last closing price. Because of this risk, swing traders often trade in smaller portions compared to day traders.

Chapter 3: Investment of Shares

Shares are units of financial assets or equity ownership in a corporation owned by investors who exchanged capital for them. There are two types of shares: common and preferred shares. Common shares offer investors corporate voting rights and profits through dividends and share price appreciation. Preferred shares, on the other hand, do not appreciate at a price. However, they do offer regular dividends and can be redeemed at an attractive price. Despite most companies having shares, only shares of public corporations can be found through the stock exchange. These corporations offer shares in exchange for financial capital that they use to operate and grow the company. More financial capital means bigger profits, leading to more shares being issued in hopes of more capital. This is an investment cycle that keeps economic markets running.

Stop-Loss Orders

Stop-loss orders are like insurance policies set in place by investors to minimize losses on their investments, as their name suggests. These orders are automated and will buy or sell securities when a certain price is reached, all of which are based on the investor's criteria. For example, a trader can implement a stop-loss order for 20% below the price the security was initially bought at. This way, if a share that was originally bought at $30 and later on drops to $24, the order in place will automatically sell the share to prevent any more financial loss to the investor. These orders are popular in swing trading to limit multiple losses over multiple shares.

These fail-safes do not require constant supervision from the trader and minimize the losses for investors. They cost nothing to implement and remove human emotion and market sentiment from influencing trades that could be unprofitable. Holding onto a favored stock and blindly hoping for an uptrend does not make a smart investor.

However, these orders are not without fault. Since they are automated and happen instantly, a short-term fluctuation in the market can cause the order to sell shares that could cause a potential uptrend in the near future. Since some shares are known to fluctuate easier than others, a slight movement in price can end in the loss of potential profitable investments. Keep in mind that there are no recommended percentages for stop-loss orders as it all depends on the individual investor. A short-term investor may set lower percentages to limit their losses on multiple fluctuating shares. In contrast, a long-term trader will set higher percentages since they understand the market fluctuations and are gaining profits through dividends and other resources. No matter the kind of investor, anyone can benefit from implementing stop-loss orders in their trading strategy.

Technical Analysis

Technical analysis is considered a trading discipline, which is used to identify trading opportunities seen through price trends and market patterns. Technical analysts will gather historical data on statistical trends gathered from previous trading activity, such as price movement and volume. This qualitative data of the market helps investors make educated assumptions about their financial securities and current investments.

Technical analysis tools are used to study the ways supply and demand for financial securities will affect changes in volume, price, and implied volatility. These tools often help generate short-term charts and patterns that can provide investors with insight into the state of various assets in the market. Since almost all tradable instruments are subject to the forces of supply and demand, price movements of stocks, bonds, etc. can be predicted with technical analysis.

There are three base market assumptions that technical analysts will make. First is the theory that the market discounts everything. This means that a company's economic fundamentals and broader market factors like market sentiment are already priced into securities. Therefore the only thing left is the analysis of price movements, which is shown through the market's supply and demand. Second, the price of securities, regardless of the time frame observed, will always follow a trend despite the random nature of the market. Meaning the price of a stock is more likely to follow a previous trend than it is to move erratically. Finally, technical analysts believe that history will inevitably repeat itself which explains the repetitive nature of price movements that are affected by market psychology. Human emotions like fear and excitement will affect market sentiment, which then affects the price of securities within their downtrend window or uptrend window.

Fundamental Analysis

Fundamental analysis is the method of measuring an asset's intrinsic value or its worth by examining the related financial and economic factors. Anything that can affect an asset's worth is analyzed and taken into consideration. Microeconomic factors like a company's internal management, macroeconomic factors including industry conditions and the market as a whole are all analyzed. All this data is examined in hopes to give the fundamental analyst a fair market value that will help determine if an asset is over or undervalued when compared to its current market price. These values are estimations to determine if an asset will either appreciate or depreciate in the near future. If an asset is deemed to be undervalued by a fundamental analyst, then that means that its current value should rise in the future to match its fair market value.

Quantitative values like income statements and balance sheets are not the only fundamental factors that come into play when determining a fair market value or, as some investors call it, the company's intrinsic value. Qualitative factors such as a company's business model, their customer base, and their local and global competition can affect an asset's intrinsic value. Market share is a popular qualitative value that represents the percentage of total sales within an economic industry generated by a specific corporation. If a company's market share is growing, that means that it is generating more revenues than its competitors. Increased market share allows for higher profitability and greater operations and business investments. Companies grow their market share by lowering prices and advertising to increase their consumer base or introducing new products and services to generate demands and revenues. This tool is used to show a company's financial market power in relations to their competitors.

As mentioned before, both technical and fundamental analysis are two major schools of thought when it comes to who views the market. The core of the technical analysis is that all known fundamentals are already factored into the price of securities meaning they hold little to no importance. Fundamentalists evaluate their securities by measuring their intrinsic value. At the same time, technical investors will instead use charts to identify patterns and trends that will predict the future price movements of financial assets.

Portfolio Diversification

Portfolio diversification is an investment strategy that attempts to limit investors' potential financial risks by having varying assets in their portfolios. This allows for their securities with positive performances to help cushion the blow of investments that are performing negatively. This works best with securities that are not correlated, or that do not belong to the same sector, as this strategy requires opposing investments that guarantee that when one asset is down another will go up.

Portfolio diversification is simple. Instead of investing all their capital into one asset class such as stocks, investors will spread out their capital into multiple investment classes, including stocks, bonds, real estate, etc. Then within each asset class, there are other means of varying a portfolio such as investing in different sectors, various market capitalizations, even investing abroad into foreign securities that are less correlated to at home market fluctuations.

Diversifying one's portfolio is very important in order to mitigate risk and potential losses while acting as a buffer for market volatility. However, this strategy also comes with its share of disadvantages. For instance, the increased amount of holding required to diversify a portfolio can increase fees relating to transactions, trading, and broker commission. It is also more time-consuming to manage a portfolio, which could mean needing to hire a portfolio manager, which is another expense. Therefore this spreading-out strategy of portfolio diversification works both ways by lessening both the reward and the risk of portfolio investments.

Chapter 4: Investing in Options and Bonds

What Are Options?

A stock option is like an investor's right to buy or sell a stock at an agreed-upon price and time; however, these are no obligations. Two types of stock options exist: a call and a put. The former is a bet that a stock's price will fall, while the latter is a bet that a stock's price will rise. Beyond the two types, there are also two styles of stock options: American and European. American options can be used anytime between the purchase and the expiration date, while European options can only be used on the expiration date and are less common than their American counterpart.

As in any form of investment, short-term and long-term stock options exist. Short-term options usually have a range of days or weeks between purchase and their expiration date. These types of options are often cheaper in price because of their low time value. They are usually placed before a major event such as a company conference, economic reports, or bigger national events like a presidential election. The nature of the event can have major effects on these options, with the value either greatly increasing afterward or decreasing to nothing. Long-term options, on the other hand, have an expiration date that is six months or more away from the purchase date. They are more expensive than their short-term counterparts. However, they require less financial capital than buying stocks in bulk allowing investors to gain leverage in a stock. Since these underlying stocks will start to use value if the stock starts to decrease, they do require appreciation in order for them to be profitable. Because their value stagnates or decreases, it is an automatic loss.

An options contract is used as the agreement between two parties to exchange capital and securities at a preset day and price. Investors must pay a premium for the rights that the contract grants. For stock options, the contract represents 100 shares of the underlying stock. Therefore, call options are leveraged bets on the appreciation of financial security, while put options are the same for depreciating stock prices.

Both options can be profitable for their respective investors. Call option buyers are assuming that the share price will rise above the purchased or strike price before the option's expiration date. If this happens, the bullish investor can use their option to buy the stocks at the strike price and immediately be able to sell them at their current price for a profit. On the other hand, call option sellers are bearish in nature since they assume the value of their shares will remain constant or depreciate. The maximum profitable income the seller of the call option will receive is the premium paid for the option. However, the seller can lose money if the value instead appreciates, as now the seller must fulfill the option by either selling their own shares or buying shares at current market value and selling those.

Put option buyers want stock prices to decrease. This is because if the market price were to drop below the strike price at expiry, the investor could utilize their put option which is to sell the shares at the option's higher price point. The profit in this scenario is the strike price minus the current market value plus expenses, which includes premiums and commissions. This result is then multiplied by the number of option contracts purchased, then again by 100, with the assumption that each contract is 100 stocks. The risk associated with buying put options is limited to the loss of the premium if the options were to expire worthlessly.

Sellers of put options are bullish writers of options contracts, meaning their maximum profit is the premium charged if the stock price closes above the strike price. However, if the value of the stocks drops below the strike price, the writer must buy the shares at the strike price, meaning the option was exercised by the buyer. The buyer sells their shares at the strike price since their value has surpassed the stock market price. Depending on how far the value has depreciated, the put seller's loss can be significant despite any cushioning the premium may provide.

What Are Bonds?

Bonds are instruments representing a loan from an investor to a borrower, who are usually corporations or organizations. They are referred to as fixed-income instruments. This is due to being traditionally paid a fixed interest rate to debtholders, however, floating or variable interest rates are now common. A bond is a sort of IOU between the lender and borrower that describes the details of the loan and its repayments. Those details also include the end date of the repayments along with either the fixed or variable interest rates. Because of this, bond rates are correlated to each other; when those rates increase, the price of the bonds decreases and vice-versa.

Corporations and governments use bonds to finance their operations and projects, while owners of these bonds are creditors or debtholders to the issuers. These loans do have expiration dates in which the principal amount needs to be paid entirely or risk default. Since both organizations often need to borrow more money than banks can provide, bonds act as a way for multiple investors to act as lenders. Hundreds to thousands of investors can all lend a portion of the borrowing amount through public debt markets. Also, through these markets, investors can also buy and sell bonds with each other even after the initial organization received their capital.

Most bonds initial pricing is usually set at par, meaning at $100 or $1,000 denominations per bond. Factors such as the credit quality of the issuer and the maturity of the loan determine the market value of bonds. Through trading bonds, investors can repurchase bonds that receive changes in either their interest rates or the issuer's credit quality.

Here are some terms that are commonly used to discuss bonds. First, there is "face value," which refers to the amount that the bond will be worth at the end of its maturity date. This amount is also used to calculate interest rate payments. Another term is coupon rate, which is the rate usually expressed as a percentage of the interest the bond issuer will pay on the face value of the bond. For example, a coupon rate of 7% for a bond of $1,000 face value means the bondholders will receive $70 per coupon date, which refers to the date that interest payments are made. These payments can be paid at any interval but semiannually is the most common.

Government and Agency Bonds

Government bonds, or treasury securities, are divided into three different categories based on their maturity and are one of the safest investments in the market. The first category is T-Bills which have the shortest maturity of the three government bonds. These bonds are issued at varying times, usually in only a matter of days, with a maximum maturity of 52 weeks. Commonly sold in denominations of $1,000, the interest rates for T-Bills depend on the length of maturity. Since these are government-issued securities, they are considered a conservative and safe investment. They can also be sold before the maturity date to another investor for a short-term gain depending on their value on the market.

The second category of treasury securities are T-Notes, which have maturity dates ranging from two to ten years. T-Notes' interest rates are fixed and depend on the length of their maturity, and their payments occur semiannually. In contrast to T-Bills, these securities are issued at par of $100, and the treasury auctions the medium-range bonds starting from one year to seven-year T-Notes on a monthly basis. At the same time, longer ten-year long-maturity bonds are auctioned on specific months through the year, often quarterly. The third category of T-Bonds follows the same guidelines as T-Notes; however, the main difference is their lengths as T-Bonds can have maturity terms of 30 years.

The main benefit of Treasury securities is that they are backed by the full faith and credit of the government. Therefore investors are guaranteed their return via both interest rates and the principal amount of the bond, as long as they are held until maturity. These bonds are also tax-exempt at the local and municipal levels. However, since these bonds are taxable at the federal level, any gains and losses need to be declared every tax season.

While Government Bonds are issued by a treasury, agency bonds are issued directly from a government department or a government-sponsored corporation. These bonds are completely backed by the government, meaning that interest rates and face value returns are guaranteed. They are often sold in increments of $10,000 and offer slightly greater interest rates than Treasury securities. The main risk for either bond is their interest rates. An investor buying such bonds in 2017 might have lower interest rates than an investor buying the same bond in 2020 and vice versa. Due to their long position nature, these bonds should match the individual investors' financial needs and wants.

Corporate Bonds

As aforementioned, corporate bonds are issued when a corporation needs capital to finance future business endeavors, and they can be bought through an equity firm, brokers, or directly on the market through online platforms. These bonds work like an IOU, with the business promising to repay the face value of the bond by a preset date along with the regular interest rate payments throughout the year. All corporate bonds come with a bond rating which aims to calculate the risk associated with each bond issue. These ratings are based on many factors such as growth potential, financial stability, and any current corporate debt. Such factors help assign letter grades to bonds which helps investors know whether or not the issuer can repay their debt or might default on their obligation. Bond ratings that are AAA to BBB are considered good investment grades, meaning they are often safer and more stable investments with low potential risk. Anything lower than a BBB is considered a junk bond.

A junk bond suggests a company with liquidity problems with potentially a higher investment risk, however, maybe bigger yields.

Since the market is ever-changing, longer bonds typically have higher interest rates in order to entice investors to agree to higher bond prices in return for more profit. Some bonds are called redeemable bonds, and these can be redeemed anytime before the maturity date. Despite the investor losing out on the continuation of the interest rate payments, the corporation does pay a premium.

Although no corporate bonds are completely risk-free due to the fluctuating market, these bonds do offer a steady income due to their interest rates over the lifetime of the bond. For financial insurance, if a business were to declare bankruptcy during the lifetime of their bonds, bondholders do have a claim on their cash and assets. These bonds help diversify portfolios and allow for a slightly more stable investment option.

Municipal Bonds

Just like with many bonds, municipal bonds refer to investors lending money to receive interest rates over the course of the bond along with the face value amount loaned at the maturity date. These bonds come both in taxable and tax-exempt formats, with the latter being the most favored. Investors seeking a tax-free income source while holding onto capital will flock to tax-exempt municipal bonds. These bonds are separated into two varieties: general obligation bonds, which are used to raise immediate funds, and revenue bonds, which are used to finance infrastructure projects. Both of these are considered low risk since issuers are almost guaranteed to honor their bonds and pay back debt.

As with the bonds previously discussed here, there are many strategies when it comes to buying and exchanging bonds in order to make capital gains. The most simple of them is to buy bonds with enticing interest rates and hold them to their maturity. This way, the investor has a steady stream of income via interest rates along with their return. Even if the bond is paid out, a premium is issued to the bondholder as a reward for the early debt retirement. Another, more complex strategy is the creation of something called a "municipal bond ladder." These ladders are a series of bonds with varying interest rates and maturity dates. When one bond matures, the original capital from the bond is reinvested into another bond, continuing the steady income. These forms of investment are considered passive due to the fact that the bonds are held until maturity and do not require much oversight. An active investor might buy bonds and sell them instead to generate profits from selling them at a premium on the market. Despite municipal bonds not being as risk-free as government bonds, they act as tax-havens that offer greater returns than their government counterparts.

Chapter 5: Mutual Funds and Precious Metals

Mutual Funds are portfolios consisting of stocks, bonds, and other securities that give investors access to portfolios that are already diversified professionally. They usually charge annual fees as well as any commissions or premiums for the money manager in charge. These mutual funds are categorized by the sectors that they represent or the combination of securities they hold. An example of such would be the majority of employer-sponsored retirement plans set by corporations.

Investors' money gets pooled into these mutual funds, which are later used to buy other securities like stocks or bonds. These investments will influence the value of the mutual fund. When an investor partakes in mutual funds, they are not investing in individual securities. Instead, they are investing in the value of the portfolio as a whole. Therefore, holders of mutual funds do not acquire any individual stock benefits such as voting rights. The price of a mutual fund is referred to as Net Asset Value per share, shortened to NAV or NAVPS. The NAV is influenced by the value of the securities that create the mutual fund. These NAVs do not fluctuate during day trading hours. Instead, they are settled at the end of market hours meaning that the value of the mutual fund is determined when the NAV is settled.

Investors' income through mutual funds is gained as annual distributions of dividends from the portfolio's stocks and bond investments. This capital can either be taken as profit or reinvested into the mutual fund. Also included in the distribution are any profits gained from selling portfolio securities. Investors can also sell their mutual funds for a profit if the NAV is higher than when they originally bought.

A mutual fund can be seen as a virtual company, with fund managers who are also usually the owners, legally forced to work in the best interest of mutual fund shareholders.

Exchange Traded Funds

An exchange traded fund, or ETF for short, is a type of security that tracks a sector, index or other asset that can then be purchased or sold on a stock exchange like a regular stock. Think of it like a basket of securities that investors can trade on an exchange, just like a regular stock. ETFs have the possibility to contain various types of investments such as financial commodities, stocks or bonds while offering lower expense ratios and commissions in comparison to buying individual stocks to trade on the market. Comparable to mutual funds, these ETFs have their prices updated throughout the day as they are bought and sold. Mutual funds instead are not traded on an exchange and only after the market is closed. Therefore exchange traded funds are considered more liquid and cost-effective than mutual funds.

There are various types of ETFs, such as Bond ETFs, which can include the government and corporate bonds aforementioned in this book. Industry ETFs track specific industries such as oil, technology and banking while currency ETFs participate in the investment of foreign currencies.

The advantages of investing into exchange traded funds are that they provide investors with lower expenses. ETFs are cheaper than buying all the individual stocks and broker commissions and transaction fees are also lessened with ETFs in comparison. Some brokers even offer no to low commissions on low-cost ETFs which helps reduce investor expenses even more. ETFs also offer access to a larger variety of holdings across sectors and industries which in turn help diversify an investment portfolio, minimizing long-term losses.

While most ETFs are considered a passive investment, there are actively-managed ETFs which involve portfolio managers buying, selling and changing the holdings within the fund. These funds are usually more costly, but they offer greater market oversight. Other disadvantages of investing into ETFs can include their lack of liquidity, which hinders their market transactions. Also, ETFs that focus on one sector or industry remove their diversification nature in financial portfolios.

Income Funds

Income funds are mutual funds or exchange-traded funds that prioritize current income instead of appreciation of values and capital gains. These funds are low-risk and often are made up of bonds, other fixed-income securities, and dividends. Just as with mutual portfolios, the share prices of these income funds are not fixed, meaning that they will fall when the market interest rates increase and vice versa. Typically these portfolios only contain investment-grade bonds, in addition to securities with sufficient credit, quality to ensure the preservation of capital.

Income Funds come in various types, depending on the types of securities invested into. Bond-Funds are normally investments of government or corporation bonds. Government bonds, as previously mentioned, are virtually low risk, which makes good investment options during a time of market uncertainty. Corporations, on the other hand, carry a slight chance that they cannot make interest payments or that they will default on the bond. Due to this risk, they often pay higher interest rates to entice investors. These bonds are classified as investment-grade or junk bonds, depending on their bond rating.

When funds are invested predominantly into stocks that have regular dividend payouts, they become known as equity income funds. These funds offer investors regular stable income via dividends generated by their portfolios. Equity income funds are a popular investment for retirees as it provides predictable profits on a monthly basis.

Index Funds

Index Funds are a kind of mutual fund or ETF that are constructed to track the components of a financial market index, which are hypothetical portfolios of investment holdings that represent a piece of the actual financial market. The value of these indexes comes from their underlying holdings, and investors use "weighting" to adjust and understand the individual impact of items in an index. Revenue-weighted and fundamental-weighting are typical examples of adjusted individual values in indexes.

Returning to index funds, these portfolios of stocks are designed to imitate the behavior and performance of a financial market index. These provide investors with low operations fees and portfolio turnover as well as broader exposure to the market as they hold various securities. A fund manager will create an index mutual fund containing holding that matches the securities of a certain index. The assumption is that if that index is faring well, so will the holdings in a similar sector. Because of this and the long-term commitment of mutual index funds, they are considered passive investments. However, they are also considered core financial portfolio investments for individual retirement accounts.

Actively managed mutual funds are usually more expensive than their passive counterparts due to their increased number of staff and market transactions. These fees can mean losses that, in the long run, compare to a passive mutual fund. However, in the short term, these actively run funds can generate greater profits. The overall low fees for mutual index funds is why they have become a popular long-term investment option for the passive investor.

Precious Metals

Precious metals are highly valuable metals because of their uses in industrial businesses and their historical role as stores of value.

Their scarcity also increases their value, making precious metals rare and valuable economic instruments. The most common precious metals for investors include silver, gold, and platinum. Specifically, gold and silver, when at least 99.5% pure, are called Bullion. Investors mainly invest in these metals as financial assets, but they also help diversify portfolios.

There are various ways to acquire stock in precious metals. One way is to purchase physical stock such as minted bars and coins; however, this incurs storage and insurance fees as well as the risk of theft. Another way is to buy future contracts of the precious metal or acquire shares in a corporation that deals in precious metals exploration and production. One can also use mutual funds to include securities in mining and such.

The Bullion market is like the stock market but for precious metals. It is where gold and silver along with other precious metals are sold, bought and traded. The London Bullion Market is the primary market of its kind, operating 24 hours a day and overseeing the futures and options trading. The few corporations with a membership to the London Bullion Market exchange gain the majority of their revenues from gold and silver. A good portion of Bullion is held in reserve in central banks, making up approximately 20% of all mined gold.

Types of Precious Metals

Gold is valued 24 hours a day, seven days a week, and is mostly unaffected by supply and demand. Instead, the price of gold is influenced by market sentiment. This is because the current hoarded supply of gold greatly outweighs the mining supply. Therefore, gold hoarders can drive the price down by supplying the market with more gold. Any new supply of gold is quickly absorbed by investors and gold hoarders alike, driving the price up. Gold hoarders include central banks that use precious metals for their many financial benefits.

Silver, like gold, is often hoarded as a store of value; however, its value changes due to its importance as an industrial metal. Because of this, the supply and demand of production industries for silver exert a heavy influence on its price. This means that the value of silver is more volatile than gold, increasing when industry demands are high while decreasing when not. Examples of this are the decrease in silver's value in the photography industry with the invention of digital cameras to the rise of silver in batteries, micro conduits markets, and technological industries.

Another precious metal traded is platinum, which is more valuable than gold because it is a rarer natural resource. Other than its rarity, additional factors determine its value. Like silver, platinum has many different industrial uses, from automobiles and jewelry to computers. Russia and South Africa have the biggest concentrations of platinum mines, and this creates issues on a global scale, such as cartel wars and market trust, that can drive prices. The automobile industry also relies heavily on platinum which drives prices up as cleaner cars are made. However, palladium, which is platinum's less expensive sister metal, could replace it, causing uncertainty for platinum's value. All these factors make this metal the most volatile out of the three.

Investing in the precious metal carries no credit risk or fear of inflation while also offering investors some form of financial insurance during political or global crises. They also help decrease the volatility and risks when incorporated in portfolios, acting as a sort of safety blanket. Through investing in mutual funds, acquiring Bullion of precious metals, and purchasing contract futures, investors can soften financial blows and gain financial security. As the value of securities fluctuates on a rapid basis, precious metals offer investors a stable store of values.

Chapter 6: Real Estate Investments

Investing in real estate can be a profitable investment; however, being a landlord requires a lot of initial capital and can come with many expenses. Landlord expenses include mortgage and property taxes, and the job itself requires one to maintain their estates, find tenants and deal with inconveniences. Being a landlord is a hands-on investment unless a property manager is hired, which is another expense of real estate investments. Choosing neighborhoods, tenants, and employees carefully will help minimize risks.

Despite the amount of work required, becoming a landlord is a profitable investment. The first form of profit is charging rent to tenants, which is determined by the value of the property and location. Charge too much rent and you will limit the number of possible tenants; charge too little and you won't maximize your profits. A rule of thumb is to charge enough to cover mortgage payments until they are paid off, at which point the majority of the rent becomes profits. Another way to generate revenues is through value appreciation. Real estate tends to appreciate in value, meaning that it can be sold at a higher price point later on. Despite this, there are no guarantees that properties will appreciate as many factors come into play when determining neighborhood and property values.

While this style of investment is more passively long-term, there are house flippers of real estate, just like the day traders of the stock market. House flippers purchase real estate for short periods of time and then resell at a higher price. How so? These real estate investors can purchase properties and then repair and update them quickly to resell them new and improved. In doing so, one has to ensure that the value will increase with these upgrades and ensure that the new price covers the capital invested enough to be profitable. Another way to profit off real estate rapidly is to buy property in a rising market and then resell it at its new valued price after a few months.

With either type of house flipping, the investor must make sure that the revenue generated will cover the costs enough to be financially beneficial. Poor construction engineering can delay repairs and increase long-term expenses. A market could not rise as much as presumed, leaving a landlord to now choose between renting the property and reselling it at a limited price.

Real Estate Groups

Real Estate Investment Trust

Real Estate Investment Trusts are companies that own, finance, and operate revenue-generating real estate properties. They invest in most real estate types such as hotels, apartments, warehouses, and more. Modeled after mutual funds, they pool the capital of many investors, allowing investors to earn dividends from their investments without needing to own, manage or finance their own properties. Most real estate investment trusts, or REITs, are publicly traded like stocks. This offers them increased liquidity compared to physical real estate. These trusts give investors a steady income via dividends; however, they have little to no means of capital appreciation.

There are three types of REITs, with the most common one being equity REITs. These are managed and owned properties that generate the majority of their income through rent and not through reselling. Then, there are mortgage real estate investment trusts that lend money to owners and operators of real estate. This capital can be borrowed directly through loans and mortgages or through the acquiring of mortgage-backed securities. The net interest margin, which is the margin between the expense of funding these loans and the charged interest rates, is what generates revenues in mortgage REITs. This makes this type of investment particularly sensitive to fluctuations in interest rates. The final type is hybrid REITs which are a combination of both aforementioned types.

Investors use both equity and mortgage strategies to generate income.

Depending on how these investments are bought and held, they can also be classified as publicly, non-publicly, or privately traded stock. Publicly traded REITs have shares that are tradable on the stock exchange, which are then bought by individual investors. These shares are regulated by governments' financial departments. As its name states, non-publicly traded REITs are still on the stock market, but they are non-tradable on national stock exchanges. Because of this, they are less liquid than their traded counterparts, but they are less susceptible to changes in the market. Private REITs, on the other hand, are not traded at all on national securities exchanges and can only be bought by institutional investors.

REITs are great additions to investment portfolios because they offer investors long-term income through dividends and diversification of securities. Since most people trade on the stock exchange, they are easy to buy and sell, which their traditional brick and mortar counterparts lack. Their liquidity, along with their attractive risk-adjusted returns, is enticing to many investors. However, they have a low potential for capital appreciation due to most of the revenue going back to investors as income instead of reinvesting in new holdings. They are also subject to market changes in addition to high management fees, transactions, and dividends being taxable income may sway investors to take their investment elsewhere.

Before moving on, real estate mutual funds must be discussed. These are mutual funds that typically will invest into real estate operations or REITs. These mutual funds offer investors a diversified exposure with a broader range of real estate investments for less financial capital than purchasing individual investment trusts. Like REITs, real estate mutual funds are pretty liquid, and they also offer analytical insight into certain real estate investments. Investing in a multitude of mutual funds with different outweighing assets and property types can give investors research information on real estate while maximizing returns.

Real Estate Investment Groups

Real Estate Investment Groups, or REIGs, are entities that focus the majority of the business investments into real estate. To generate profits, these groups will either buy, renovate, sell or invest in properties. Commonly they will purchase a property and rent units to other investors while staying in charge of administration and maintenance. These real estate investment groups also usually do not qualify for REIT status, meaning they are not held down by real estate regulations and requirements.

REITs are made up of multiple partners and shareholders who pool together their financial capital in order to make greater and broader investments. Since only the majority of their business needs to be in real estate, they have flexibility in their internally structured and make investments as desired. REITs will often lease properties to real estate management companies or clients in exchange for a portion of the rent. They can also sell units of the property but still maintain overall control. Since there are no true limitations on REIGs' business activities, they are often marketed as real estate investment groups to attract investors.

The structure of these groups is commonly a partnership or a corporation. The former is a partnership of two or more investors who share profits, losses, and expenses, and their stakes are usually proportional to their investments. Depending on the structure of the partnership, some are more collaborative, while others have members who do not participate in the daily business aspects. However, these partners still receive their profits, voting rights, and other partnership perks outlined in their contracts. The latter, on the other hand, is the formation of either a public or private corporation. Incorporating a business allows its shares to be traded for equity which helps fund operations and reinvestments. Because of this, however, they are regulated by financial departments, and public equity is subject to value fluctuation along with the market while private equity is valued privately. Online real estate platforms now allow for crowdfunding which allows for accredited and non-accredited investors to pool capital for investments. These follow the same structure as partnerships.

Similarly, real estate limited partnerships, or RELPs, are similar to real estate investment groups because they both are entities that buy and hold a property or portfolios of properties. These partnerships, however, only last a limited amount of years. The general partner is usually a real estate development firm or a property manager. Whoever it is, they seek out financial capital from other investors who then become limited partners. During the partnership, the partners all receive the periodic income generated through the RELPs properties. However, the biggest gain is from the selling of actual properties followed by the partnership dissolving in the future.

Why Invest in Real Estate

Generally speaking, the real estate market has low volatility, especially when compared to other securities like bonds and equities. It also has somewhat of a negative correlation with other financial assets. In most cases, when stock values are low, real estate is high. This allows for portfolio diversification and protection against the risks of other securities. More direct real estate investments allow for a better hedge, which means using multiple financial securities to offset price changes and minimize risk. Less direct investments such as REITs or real estate mutual funds are always going to reflect the market and therefore offer less in terms of portfolio hedging.

However, all real estate investments have an inflation hedging capability. This is due to the positive relationship real estate has with a country's GDP, or Gross Domestic Product. The expansion of economies increases the demand for real estate, which drives up prices and, in turn, means higher capital. Thus, real estate maintains purchasing power of capital and redistributes inflation onto tenants, and incorporates some through capital appreciation.

One investment tool only found in real estate, with the exception of REITs, is leverage. When buying stocks, one must pay the full value of the stock at the time of purchase. However, with mortgages, investors can have multiple real estate investments that are not all paid for. Most mortgages ask for a 20% down payment; however, those down payments can be as low as 5%. Despite not paying for the property in full, the investor owns and has full control of it as soon as the papers are signed. This entices house flippers and landlords because they use mortgages and acquire multiple properties without having the total valued capital. With full control of these assets, investors can rent out units, hold to resell, and renovate to increase the value, which all contribute to profits in the long run despite only having paid a portion of the total value.

As with any investments, real estate does have its downsides. Since it is hard to convert immediately into cash, it is considered illiquid, with real estate transactions taking up to multiple months to complete. While REITs and real estate mutual funds do offer better liquidity and follow the value of the market, they are more volatile. They also offer less portfolio diversification since they are more correlated to the market compared to direct real estate investments.

Whether directly investing, taking on the duties of a landlord, or participating in real estate groups, real estate can be a profitable investment. This is a financial investment with the potential to provide investors with a regular steady income. With realistic expectations of the labor involved and tons of prior research, real estate investors can greatly increase their personal wealth.

Conclusion

Investing can be scary, but it should not be. Historically, it seemed as if only those with established financial ties could participate in the market. The abundance of economic terms, confusing graphs, and lack of access to investment knowledge can push potential investors away. All the numbers, market variables, fluctuations, and risks associated with it make it seem like a concept only knowledgeable people can participate in. However, if you are reading this part of the book, you know that anyone and everyone can invest. No matter the age, experience or financial capital of the trader.

Now it is time to do some personal exploration and reflection. Are you an active day-trader who can weather the potential risks for an even bigger reward? Or are you a buy-and-hold type of investor with future goals that these investments will benefit from? Do you know what sector to invest in, or would you rather hire someone to build you a professional financial portfolio and increase your chance of success? All these questions need to be answered in order to create the perfect investment strategy that is molded to your personal goals and desires. Finding out what investments works for you and which ones do not is part of the process.

Now, you have the instruments necessary to take that first leap in the world of investments. You can now incorporate short and long-term investments in your financial portfolio to boost your economic standing. You know how to save, invest and grow your wealth through not only the stock market but also through precious metals, real estate, and mutual funds. This book has given you a foundation of investment knowledge, and now you can be a more comfortable investor.

So does one need to be a financial expert to trade and invest? Absolutely not.

References

Anderson, A. (2019). Investing: Invest Like A Pro: Stocks, ETFs, Options, Mutual Funds, Precious Metals and Bonds. Lulu.com.

Chen, J. (2019). Primary Market. Investopedia. https://www.investopedia.com/terms/p/primarymarket.asp

Chen, J. (2020, December 31). Contrarian Definition. Investopedia. https://www.investopedia.com/terms/c/contrarian.asp

Cussen, M. P. (2019, March 19). Introduction to Treasury Securities. Investopedia. https://www.investopedia.com/articles/investing/073113/introduction-treasury-securities.asp

Frey, A. H. (2013). A beginner's guide to investing : how to grow your money the smart and easy way. Ivy Bytes.

Investopedia. (2010). Bond Basics Tutorial. http://i.investopedia.com/inv/pdf/tutorials/bondbasics.pdf

Investopedia. (2020a, August 31). A Real Estate Investing Guide. Investopedia. https://www.investopedia.com/mortgage/real-estate-investing-guide/

Investopedia. (2020b, September 5). Active vs. Passive Investing: What's Best for You? Investopedia. https://www.investopedia.com/news/active-vs-passive-investing/

Kenton, W. (2019). Secondary Market. Investopedia. https://www.investopedia.com/terms/s/secondarymarket.asp

Kramer, M. (2020, July 1). Over-The-Counter Market Definition. Investopedia. https://www.investopedia.com/terms/o/over-the-countermarket.asp

Langager, C. (2019). A Beginner's Guide to Stock Investing. Investopedia. https://www.investopedia.com/articles/basics/06/invest1000.asp

Laopodis, N. T. (2020). Understanding Investments: Theories and Strategies (2nd ed.). Routledge. https://doi.org/10.4324/9781003027478

SEC, & UNITED STATES - SECURITIES AND EXCHANGE COMMISSION. (2010). Mutual Funds A Guide for Investors Information is an investor's best tool. https://www.sec.gov/investor/pubs/sec-guide-to-mutual-funds.pdf

U.S. Securities and Exchange Commission. (n.d.). Saving and Investing for Students. Retrieved April 23, 2021, from https://www.sec.gov/investor/pubs/savings-investing-for-students.pdf

Young Investors Society. (2016). Stock investing 101. Yis.org; Young Investors Society. https://yis.org/wp-content/uploads/2016/10/Stock-Investing-101-eBook.pdf

Passive Income – Beginners Guide

Proven Business Models and Strategies to Become Financially Free and Make an Additional $10,000 a Month

Joel Jacobs

Introduction

When you are working for someone else, they have control over your pay. Even if you have been working the same job for ten or more years, keeping this job is never guaranteed. The company you work for could get sold, go bankrupt, or decide to move locations, leaving you suddenly unemployed and without pay. What's worse, depending on the job market and your professional career, finding another job may not be quickly accomplished. For this reason, and among others, more and more people are turning to 'side hustles' to bring in a second income.

A passive income stream allows you to generate a line of income separate from your day job. "Passive income" refers to earnings that require little to no effort to earn or maintain—like a rental property or other enterprises where you do not have to be actively involved in operations. It gives you a little extra security and relief knowing that whatever happens with your 9 to 5, you won't have to worry about paying bills or putting food on the table. With a passive income stream, you can be as active or passive as you wish. You can put the work in once and then allow some money to trickle in for months and years later. Alternatively, you can maintain a profitable business that allows you the freedom to live the life you have always dreamed of.

This book is designed to simplify the process of getting started and maintaining a passive income. Whether you have a demanding career already or are staying home to raise your children, anyone can create a passive income. Learn how to generate more money each month to set aside for a rainy day, quit your day job, or put towards your future home. To truly have financial freedom, you need to have money coming from more than one source. Many of the ideas in this book require little or no upfront investment, so you don't have to wait until you save up enough to get started. You can use the information in this book today and benefit from starting now in just a few months. The process is not complex, and you can easily take advantage of multiple passive income streams so you won't have to worry about being financially strained again.

Chapter 1: Affiliate Marketing

Affiliate marketing has the potential to bring in 300 to 10,000 dollars a day. It is one of the most effective ways to start a passive income stream that can continuously grow for years. There are multiple ways to get started and platforms you can use to generate an affiliate marketing business. We start with this option because the information in this chapter can help you easily expand into other passive income opportunities.

What is Affiliate Marketing

Affiliate marketing is one of the most popular ways for anyone to make a steady income. You, the affiliate, find products you already enjoy using and promote them. Each time you contribute to a sale of the products, you make a commission. Products can be physical objects or services; there is also the potential to earn a small commission by promoting a company or brand. Commissions are tracked by using an affiliate link. There are a few ways to make a commission:

- Pay-per-sale — This is the standard method of earning for affiliate markers. With this approach, you earn a percentage of the sales when an individual clicks on your link. The person must purchase the product or service you are promoting to be compensated.
- Pay-per-lead — This method does not have to result in the sale of a product, but does involve the consumer performing a specific action. Pay-per-lead affiliates need to convince viewers to click on the link they provide and supply additional information for a company or brand. This typically gets viewers to sign up for a mailing list, subscribe to a social page, or download a digital product. You make a commission based on how many people complete the desired call to action.

- Pay-per-click — With pay-per-click affiliate marketing, you earn a percentage each time you drive traffic to a merchant's website. The more web traffic you can redirect to the merchant's site, the more you can earn.

Affiliate Marketing Platforms

Blogging

Starting a blog is straightforward; you create content, hit publish, and do your best to get more readers every day. Blogs are an easy way to establish many affiliate links, as you can create different posts that review or promote multiple products. The key to being successful is to grow your reach organically. You want your content to rank high on Google search engines; this requires investing a bit more time learning proper search engine optimization.

How to get started:

1. First, decide what your blog will be about. Will it be a lifestyle blog, crafting corner, health and fitness-related, or other more specific topics. Choose something that you are familiar with and can continuously create content around.
2. Think of a catchy name for your blog. You want something short and memorable. You can include your name if you plan to create a brand around yourself, making it easier to sell products.
3. Once you have decided on a few name contenders, you need a hosting site —Bluehost, HostGator, GoDaddy. Most of these offer a free domain name with the hosting plan.
4. You need a blogging platform. WordPress is the most popular for bloggers, and you can set up ecommerce options.
5. Now, you are ready to customize your blog. You can use plenty of free themes with WordPress, or you can opt to buy a theme. Each can be customized to align with your own style.

6. After you are satisfied with the look, you need to get some content written. Many start with an introductory post that lets readers know what the blog is about, who they are, and what they can expect. You want to have a posting schedule and stick with it. If you say you will post two times a week, pick two days to publish a new blog on those days. Readers are more likely to keep checking in with what you post when they can expect new content to take in. When writing your post, always end it with an open-ended question that will encourage readers to leave comments. This is important as it gets your content in higher rankings.

7. Create an email list generator. This will help you capture readers' information to let them know when you have a new post and other products that may interest them.

8. Once you have grown your audience, you can begin selling ad space on your blog. Also, consider other products or services that your audience wants to learn more about and are willing to pay for.

Podcasting

If writing content isn't your thing, but you have a knack for public speaking, podcasting might be your ticket into affiliate marketing. There are plenty of platforms that you can use to help set up your own podcast, but this option does require a little bit more of an investment in obtaining the right equipment. Like blogging, you will need a podcast hosting platform to publish content on. The following suggestions are great for beginners as they not only provide you with the right tools to get your podcast up and running, they are easy to use.

- Podbean
- BuzzSprout
- Blubrry Podcasting
- Transistor

- Smart Podcast Player
- Soundcloud

When choosing a hosting platform, you want to pay special attention to the file size and storage you are allotted. Podbean offers unlimited storage, and you can promote your podcast through various services. You still need a website and domain name to make it easier for the listener to find your content. Your website does not have to be complex. You can do this the same way you set up a blog, but will need to install the podcast WordPress plugin. Once you have this setup, you can begin recording your content.

The most important piece of equipment you will need to get started is a microphone. There are plenty of podcasting kits that come with a microphone and additional accessories that you will need, such as a shock mount to reduce noise and a mic arm for easy maneuvering while you are recording. You will also need a quality headset. You do not need to worry about investing in the best equipment, but you need to use a microphone that will lead to smooth recording. Do not use your camera's built-in microphone.

Now that you have the equipment, you can begin to plan your first episode. You want to have an outline of what you will be covering during that episode. To do this, you need to consider how long your episodes will be. There are no rules for the length of your podcast episodes need to be, your audience and content will be the determining factors. Some podcasts are under 10 minutes long; others record hour-long episodes that their audiences love.

Write a script to follow once you have an outline complete. This will help you better plan your episodes to account for pauses and will help you sound more professional. With your script, you are ready to record. To record, you will want podcast recording software that will allow you to record and edit your content. Audacity is free software that many podcast beginners use.

Consider what your intro and outro will be. If you are using music, you want to ensure that it is licensed-free. A few places to look for music include:

- Free Music Archive
- YouTube Audio Library
- Free Stock Music
- Envato Market
- SoundCloud

When you are satisfied with your first episode, you can upload it to your podcasting platform. Choose a catchy title and create a captivating description that includes a few high searched keywords to draw more attention to your episodes.

You can monetize your podcast the same way you can a blog. You can reach out to businesses to gain direct sponsorships, promote products or services through affiliate marketing, or sell your own products and services. You can transform older content for a membership or subscription option for listeners. Additionally, ask listeners to donate to your podcast by adding a donation option on your website.

Influential Marketing

Influential marketing is another type of affiliate marketing that can bring in hundreds and thousands of dollars. An influencer can use the same commission methods in traditional affiliate marketing— pay per click, pay per lead, and pay per sale. Where influencers make serious money is from campaigns. These tend to be a series of marketing posts where the influencer and brand collaborate. These campaigns can be composed of reviews, unboxings, live video and how-to's, or images showing their brand or product in daily use.

Becoming an influencer is a bit more challenging. You need to have a social presence with a large following. Many companies are seeking out influencers that not only have a huge following but, more importantly, are viewed as an expert or authority figure in their domain. Some influencers have a small following, but their following is incredibly loyal. These influencers are valuable to companies or brands looking to gain traction in a new market or with a different audience than they typically promote to.

TikTok and Instagram are the two social platforms where brands are closely looking for the best influencers. You can take matters into your own hands and reach out to companies that you already love. There are also influence marketing platforms that allow you to create portfolios, pitch campaign ideas, and begin collaborating with brands seeking out influencers. Most influencer platforms only cater to businesses or brands looking for individuals to collaborate with. There are a select few that allow influencers to create profiles to be viewed by companies for consideration. These include:

- Afluencer
- Upfluence
- ShoutCart (for Instagram influencers)
- Social Bond
- Grapevine (for YouTube, Instagram, and Facebook influencers)
- AspireIQ

Pros and Cons

There are many reasons why creating a passive income from affiliate marketing is appealing, but there are also some drawbacks to be aware of.

One perk of affiliate marketing is you don't have to worry about customer support or supplying the products. The brand or company you get the affiliate link from has to handle all the customer relations. You just need to direct the customers to them. This is also a flexible income. You can work from anywhere, set your own goals for what you want to make. The effort you put in has the biggest impact on what you earn.

The cons are few, and relate more to the outside work you need to generate a substantial income stream. You need to have a platform with a loyal audience base. To attract these followers, you need to implement proper SEO, such as searching for relevant keywords, knowing where to place them, and increasing engagement. This will get your content ranked higher, which increases the number of views and possible clicks the content will attract.

The one set back; to generate a substantial income, you have to put the time into creating valuable content. Whether you are making videos or blog posts, you need to publish engaging, memorable, and valuable content. This is not something everyone has the time to do. While technically, you only have to post content containing the affiliate link once, you need to continuously publish content that keeps your page active.

Chapter 2: Network Marketing

If you love meeting new people and share everything on social media, network marketing is an ideal passive income stream for you. The key to success with this passive income stream is to be your genuine self. Your personality and charisma will attract others to buy and join you on this passive income journey.

What is Network Marketing

Multi-level marketing (MLM) is a network marketing business model where you 'work' for a company selling goods or services. You often build a team of independent sales representatives who sell the same products or assist in closing sales. You make a commission of the products you sell and, depending on the company, you make a bonus from how well the rest of your team does. Some businesses operate on this multi-level tier system, or they may just have you sell products without recruiting. With the combination of a tier system and sale of products, there is potential to make a decent income and how much you make depends on your own effort. With most businesses, those who started early and are at the top of the tier tend to make the most money as they bring in more commissions from their downlines (the people they recruited) and anyone who gets added from the people they add. This is not the case with all network marketing businesses. In some, it does not matter when you get added to someone else's downline; you can outearn the person who recruited you if you build a team of motivated individuals who build a significant team for themselves. If the person who added you only slowly adds more people to their team and does not focus on product sales, you can outearn them.

Beware of Pyramid Schemes

MLMs can be pyramid schemes, but there are characteristics of pyramid schemes that will help you identify which is legitimate and which is not. First, pyramid schemes are often illegal business models. These focus primarily on recruiting individuals and convincing them to pay an upfront cost for a starter kit or pay for training sessions before they can get started. This is how the company makes most of its money. They are not concerned about selling products but only about recruiting more people. Many of the individuals spam everyone they know to get more salespeople under their name. Typical pyramid schemes make it impossible for you to out-earn the person who recruited you.

Finding Reputable Companies

Many reputable MLM companies have single and multi-tier systems. Those with single-tier systems tend to be safer to join, but a few have well-established tier structures that do not limit how much you can make. Some companies you may already be aware of include:

- Avon
- Mary Kay
- Excell Communications
- Tupperware
- Beachbody
- Amway
- Herbalife

It is best to research a company before committing. You want to ensure that the business is encouraging the sales of products and not just recruiting salespeople. Check the history of the company; have they been accused of being a pyramid scheme? Also, consider the products. Are the products you will have to sell ones that you use or foresee yourself using? It will be much easier to promote the products if you are enthusiastic about them.

Generating Income

Most network marketers make a few hundred dollars a month, while others have made six figures a year. Aside from having a highly social personality, creating a steady income from this option does require some innovative business sense. You need to attract people to the products and services you are selling, while also finding individuals who will build their own team from the opportunity. This can involve more of your time, but there are many ways that you can automate some aspects of the process. A few tips to keep in mind:

- Build a team from your customers. If you want to get others to sign up under you, they should already love the product and services themselves. Trying to present a business opportunity to someone who does not know about what they are expected to sell will get you many no's. Focus on selling the products, then keep an eye on the people who naturally talk about what they are using. These people are already doing what needs to be done to build a team of their own, and a majority of that is to share and get others interested.
- Host parties. Take advantage of using technology to your advantage to gather a larger group of people to present the product and service to. Online parties allow you to invite others and them to invite people they know. You can have giveaways and special offers for those who buy.
- Social media marketing is a core component of marketing products. You want your friends and their friends to know what you are offering. Take the time to understand how algorithms work and how you can get your content viewed by a larger number of users.

Pros and Cons

Many companies require some type of investment, either purchasing their products to sell or paying a business fee each month. It can be hard to identify which companies are legitimate for this reason. You must do your research before you sign up as a representative.

You may need to keep your own inventory. So companies require you to purchase a small inventory to sell, which can take up a lot of space in your home. It can also mean getting stuck with a wide range of items that you do not intend on using or can sell.

It is highly competitive, and people have gotten so used to being 'sold' that they often ignore new friend requests or invites. The business you go with can impact how resistant others will be; most people don't mind getting invited to a makeup party or Tupperware show, but sharing weight loss products can get a lot of negative feedback.

Getting started can take a lot of time and effort. Trying to sell and build a team at the same time can become overwhelming. It can also take months before you start earning money; as a general rule, most people need to be presented with an offer a minimum of five times before saying yes. Many people quit before they have even given themselves a chance to build a legitimate income.

Those who have the patience and determination can make five to six figures a year while cutting down on the time they dedicate to their business. Many have found it possible to gradually build their income while only working their business in small pockets of time throughout the day.

Chapter 3: Dropshipping

Dropshipping has been around for many years. It offers individuals a low-cost business model that can bring in big returns. It takes time, and more maintenance is involved, but it can be a highly successful revenue stream. Dropshipping allows you to open your own store without having to handle any physical products yourself. You often set up an online store and find a third-party seller who will then fulfill orders purchased on your online store.

Creating a Market Strategy

Market research is essential for finding products and understanding your target audience. You can search for trending products to include in your store. Ones that are currently selling well are a great starting point. With a bit of searching, you can find products on their way to best selling status. These products get you ahead of competitors and help you take advantage of lower marketing fees. Some resources to make use of to help identify trending products include:

- Kickstarter
- Wish
- Google Trends

Another way to find the right products is to identify a target market. This can help you narrow down your product options while also serving a large enough audience such as dog lovers, nurses, crafters. Take advantage of seasonal trends as well. Narrowing down a niche market can result in less competition, and your marketing efforts will not cost as much since you are targeting a small group of people. It is a good idea to start in a smaller niche. Once you have established a successful store with that market, you can expand to attract new customers that might not initially fall into your niche market.

Look at what your competitors are doing. Do not limit this research to products and prices. You want to try to identify their sales strategy, which can help you uncover products they may add to their stores. You may not be able to add the same products to your ecommerce store at the same price as your competitors. You might want to hold off on adding these items until you have established your store and created your unique brand.

Think outside the box when searching for products. Many people post product-related videos; this can be a way to spot trending products. If a video has had comments, shares, or likes in the past three days, this can be a good candidate product to add to your store. While you are looking for videos on your social sites, do a quick search of the social media shopping platform.

By doing these searches, you gain a substantial list of items you want to begin selling in your store.

Finding Suppliers

You can find wholesalers and manufacturers to stock your online store by using a dropshipping supplier directory. If you already know the product or at least the niche you want to sell, this will take little time to find the right supplier. Some of the best suppliers include (Ferreira, 2021):

- Oberlo
- DropnShop
- Cj Dropshipping
- Supplymedirect
- CROV

To simplify the process, you can set up your ecommerce store with a site that automatically connects you with reputable suppliers.

Creating an Online Store

Shopify is a widely used site that allows individuals to set up an online store and connects shop owners directly with supplies. They have integrated the Oberlo marketplace that helps you find products to sell, which you can import to display in your store. When someone purchases an item from your Shopify store, you just need to ensure all the information is correct on the customer order form. You approve the order, and the product is shipped directly to the customer from the supplier.

Oberlo allows you to track how much inventory a third-party supplier has. When they run out of a particular item that you may offer in your store, you can quickly take action to either remove that item or mark it as temporarily unavailable.

Generating Traffic

Driving traffic to your store is essential to a successful dropshipping business. You can do this in several ways. You can promote products on your social media account and by word of mouth. If you have a blog, YouTube channel, or podcast, you can include ads to your site to attract more customers from your followers.

While you need little money to get started in dropshipping, you will need to spend on marketing to get customers to your store. Many successful dropshippers recommend allocating at least $500 to marketing costs when you first start an ecommerce store (Ferreira, 2021).

Pros and Cons

You do not have to purchase inventory with a dropshipping business. You can set up an ecommerce store with minimal upfront starting costs. You also have a wide range of products you can sell.

There is less risk involved because you don't have to purchase inventory. You won't have to deal with the stress of unloading items that you can't sell. With traditional retail businesses, you often have a stockpile of items that you need to sell. You do not need to worry about products that are not selling. If an item is not selling well, you can remove it from your online store without loss.

There are fewer costs to starting a dropshipping business. Since you do not have to keep a physical inventory, you do not need to invest in a warehouse to store supplies or choose a physical location to sell your item. You also do not have to keep track of inventory. This means you will not have to spend time counting and managing what you sell. Even as your business grows, the cost of operating your dropshipping store remains significantly lower than a brick-and-mortar store.

You can operate a dropshipping business from just about anywhere. All you need to keep your business going is a computer/laptop and quality internet service.

The convenience and flexibility of starting a dropshipping business make it an enticing business venture. While this is great for those wanting to start their own business, this also means it can be highly competitive. With low starting costs and ease of setting up an online store, many people and even companies have dropshipping businesses and sell products at a substantially low price.

Since you are not stocking your own inventory, you have to rely on the third-party seller to have your products available. Almost all third-party sellers supply the same products to other business owners, which means that what they have to provide can change daily. It is not easy to see how much inventory the supplier has, resulting in delays while fulfilling orders.

Shipping costs can become confusing. You can set up your ecommerce store to automatically add shipping costs to a customer's order, making things easy. Unfortunately, with a dropshipping business, you will be working with multiple third-party sellers. A customer can purchase two or more items from your store, and each of these items may come from a different supplier; this means your customer now has two or more different shipping costs. It is not the best idea to pass all these shipping costs onto the customer. You can set up an automatic flat shipping fee, but calculating these can be complex. Setting a price that is too low can result in losing money.

While you don't have to handle any shipping or order fulfillment tasks, you will have to take responsibility for when things do not ship right. If your supplier forgets to include an item you will have to handle the customer service and apologize to the customer. You also do not have much control over packaging. Low-quality packaging can damage products or disappoint buyers.

Along with this lack of control over packing and shipping, there is little room to brand your own business. Many of the products you supply will carry the supplier's branding. If you do want to include your own branding on items, most suppliers will require a minimum order to be placed.

Chapter 4: Selling on Amazon

Amazon is one of the biggest ecommerce stores around, and you can start selling and earning through Amazon a few ways. Many think of selling products as the only option to selling on Amazon, but if you are a creative person, there are even more possibilities.

Fulfillment By Amazon (FBA)

Fulfill by Amazon (FBA) allows you to sell products and keep a stock inventory in Amazon's fulfillment center. Amazon will then ship, pack, and provide customer service for all items you sell. This allows you the perks of having an ecommerce store without having to worry about all these other details.

Setting up a Seller Account

You can have an Individual plan or Professional plan. With an Individual plan, you pay a flat rate each time you sell an item. With a Professional plan, you pay a monthly fee no matter how many or few items you sell. On top of these fees, Amazon also takes a portion of each sale as a 'referral fee'. This fee will fluctuate depending on the category the time is sold under.

You can sell on Amazon by reselling items, manufacturing your own product/brand to sell, or if you have a Shopify account, you can link your products to be sold on Amazon. There are restrictions to what you can sell, however. The product, category, and brand may impact whether you can sell a particular item or not. Some products are prohibited for sale, others may require special permission to list, and a few do not allow for third-party selling.

You can use a business email to start a new Amazon seller account or your current Amazon customer account to sign up. The items you plan to sell may determine which account you want to set up. To create a seller account, you will need:

- Active credit card
- Government ID
- Tax information
- Phone number
- Bank account

Pros and Cons

You can stay up-to-date with your seller account via the Amazon Seller app. The app makes it even more convenient to establish a profitable side business. With the app, you can track your sales, fulfill orders, find additional items to sell, update and edit product images, and add new items to sell.

After the initial time spent searching for and listing products, the business is relatively easy to maintain. Most profitable sellers on Amazon spend between 5 to 20 hours maintaining their business each week. On average, a third of new sellers have seen profits of over $4,000 within the first three months and have seen this income grow, reaching five figures within the first one or two years (Connolly, 2021).

You do need to invest money and time. Many sellers saw success investing around $500 into their Amazon business, and saw more success with getting their products listed than others who spent well over that amount (Connolly, 2021). The biggest issue is that you need to spend time researching products and creating listings at first. Product research is crucial to success.

EBook Publishing

If you have a knack for writing, publishing books online can lead to a hefty passive income. This is truly a passive income stream because once you do the initial work of writing and designing a book, there is little maintenance needed afterward. This is not to say that publishing just one book will generate $10,000, but publishing multiple high-quality books does have the potential to make you money for years. This is ideal for monetizing the content on other platforms for those who already have blogs, YouTube channels, or podcasts.

There are also multiple avenues to publish electronically, including Amazon Kindle Direct Publishing, Kobo, Smashwords, and Draft2Digital. These platforms each have their own benefits and drawbacks. For example, if you publish with Amazon, you get higher royalties, but they retain exclusive distribution. Smashwords, Kobo, and Draft2Digital have lower royalties, but allow you to distribute through other platforms and avenues. This means that your profit per unit may be a tad smaller, but your overall possible sales is higher. You also may wish to consider what markets are most important to you. Amazon is the biggest player in the American market, but Kobo holds a large chunk of sales in Canada and Europe.

Doing a little research will help you identify the best niche to focus on. Some of the best selling eBooks fall into the following categories:

- Business/Investing
- Computer and tech
- Health, fitness, and dieting
- Self-help
- Parenting and relationships

Before you begin to jump into the writing process, you want to ensure there is an audience for the book you write. You can do a quick search for books that may be similar to yours already for sale on Amazon. To find out what books are selling best on Kindle, you can search the "Amazon Kindle eBooks Best Sellers and More" category. You can do the same with Kobo and Apple Books by searching your intended category. It will automatically sort by bestseller. This also helps you identify your competitors. Reading the reviews of bestseller books will give you an advantage of what to include or not include in your own books.

Once you have taken the time to search for similar titles, you want to learn if there is a big enough audience buying these books. Using the same process as mentioned previously, search for your book's category under "Amazon Kindle eBooks Best Sellers and More." Click on the books that are the most similar to your idea and look under the product details. You will see the Amazon Best Sellers Rank; the number next to this is the most important. If the book has a number below 1,000, it has a high number of sales, but it also means that it's a very competitive title. If the book has a number between 1,000 to 30,000, it has done well selling copies, and there is less competition. If the book ranks above 30,000, the sales are not great, but there is also very little competition. The sweet spot is that middle range (1,000 to 30,000). With these rankings, you can feel more confident that your book will do well in this category, and there is less competition to fight against to get higher sales.

Once you have taken these first two steps, you want to honestly evaluate how your book idea will fare against the top of this category. When you first launch your book, breaking the top three in your category will ensure your books get plenty of exposure. They are listed first in the New Release section.

Professional Tips

Title — The title is the most important component of your book. You can write the best content there is, but it won't make you any money if you have a bad title. Your title needs a main title and a subtitle. The main title needs to capture potential readers' attention. It needs to be memorable while also hinting at the book's topic. The subtitle should explain how the book will help the reader. Consider what problem the book solves and how their life will change once they finish the book. A subtitle that covers these key points will intrigue the audience. To draw in more attention, use sensory words in your subtitle that will help it stand out, such as:

- Vibrant
- Delicious

- Nutritious
- Cringeworthy
- Monotonous

Cover Design — After the title, the cover design is the most crucial aspect of your book. The cover is the first impression audiences get of the content and quality of the book. A poor cover design will get overlooked every time. Successful cover designs contain two crucial components:

1. The title is clear and easy to read. Potential readers will see just a thumbnail of your book design first, and they need to be able to read the title from this thumbnail. You need to use the right typeface and font size to ensure that your title is clear and legible, even on a smaller scale.
2. It uses bold colors, an exciting image, or a careful balance of both. The cover design needs to stand out and capture the audience's attention immediately.

You can certainly attempt to create your own cover design if you have design experience. It is much better to hire a professional to create one for you. Sites like Fiverr can match you with a professional designer to create a gorgeous cover with very little investment. Be sure to look through samples of the individual's work before hiring them. Other places you can try for professional cover designs include:

- Upwork
- Happy Self Publishing
- 99 Designs
- BookBaby
- EBook Launch
- Deviant Art

The prices and packages offered with the above option will vary, but is well worth the cost, considering an amazing cover design is key to generating higher sales.

Description — The first thing customers are going to read from you is the description of the book. The description needs to sell your book; it needs to be compelling and persuade customers to buy what you have written. Your description should summarize key points of your book that benefit the reader. There should be bullet points that touch on the problems the book will solve without giving away how it solves the problem. To write a persuasive book description that will get customers to buy, consider the following tips:

1. The first sentence of the description is the most essential component. It needs to hook the reader by telling them what problem your book will solve for them.
2. Add one or two "what if" statements to get the reader to imagine what their life would be like once their problem is solved. Does the information allow them more free time, money, productivity, better relationships? Tap into the readers' pain points and help them envision a better life because of the solution they will find in the pages of your book.
3. Show your authority. Even if you don't have a degree or best-selling credentials, there are ways you can tell your reader they can trust you as an authority figure. How has the information helped you transform your life?
4. Don't ask them to take action; tell them. When writing their book description, many make a huge mistake by asking the reader to buy, when they should simply say, "Get your copy today."

Marketing — Before you launch your book, you need to have a solid plan to generate hype around your book. Have a list of people who will read and write reviews; they should also promote your book on their social media accounts. Let these individuals know that you are giving them an advanced copy of the book and when they should write the review. If you can come up with a list of 50 people, you should garner about 25 reviews by the time you launch. This gets your book ranking higher when it first launches.

Next, you want to start dropping hints about your book on your social media accounts. This builds anticipation around the launch. If you have a blog, you want to start dropping hints to your readers and mention the launch to your email list. You don't want to start pushing sales; just bring awareness to the launch.

Around two to four weeks before you launch your book, it's a good idea to send out free samples to those on your mailing list. This can be the introduction to the book or a snippet of one of the chapters.

Publish your book on your preferred platform a week before the launch date. This gives the people you sent an advanced copy time to write their reviews. If you get at least 10 reviews, you can take advantage of using book promotion sites. These early views can end up giving you a massive boost in early sales.

Pricing — There are four options when choosing the right price point to start selling your book at. You can increase or decrease the price at any time. Each time your book sells, you get a percentage of royalty fees. These are broken down as follows:

- You will get 35% of the royalty for books priced between $.99 to $2.98.
- You get 70% of royalty fees for books priced between $2.99 to $9.99.
- You get 35% of royalty fees for books priced at $10.00 and above.
- If you enroll your book in Amazon's Kindle Unlimited program, you get a percentage based on the number of pages read each month.

Many people automatically gravitate to pricing their book between $2.99 and $9.99 because they receive the highest royalties at this price point. This can be a huge mistake when you first launch your book. At the launch of your book, you want to generate the most sales; pricing your book at just $.99 can help accomplish this. The more sales you get at the start of your launch, the higher your ranking will be. It does not matter that your book is only $.99; what matters is that it is selling.

Starting with a low price has additional benefits. You can use this as an incentive for readers who have not purchased yet to get their copy before the price goes up. This also helps you get your book featured on promotional book sites like Book Bub and BookSends. These sites will promote your book while it is either available for free or $.99. Keep in mind, many of the sites require a subscription fee, but the fee is worth it to gain sales outside of Amazon. When individuals from these sites purchase your book, Amazon recognizes this and views your book as profitable. Amazon will then promote your book for free.

Promotions — Kindle Unlimited and Kobo allow you to set up promotion days where your book is offered at a discount or for free. This can be a great way to generate sales during the first two to three days of the launch and months after the launch. When it comes to generating a steady stream from publishing on your platform, you need to promote your book continuously. This will remind readers who have not purchased the book that is still available and inform new readers that you have published a book. You can entice more people to buy your book before you increase the price. When increasing the price, do it in increments to take advantage of a boost in sales.

Pros and Cons

Publishing your books is entirely free. There are no upfront costs or listing fees you need to worry about. This makes getting started easy, and there is no risk of losing money with this business venture.

Writing a book is not as easy as it appears. You need to spend time writing quality content, edit it thoroughly, and have an eye-catching cover design. On top of this, you need a marketing strategy. As nice as it would be to publish a book and let the money roll in, that doesn't happen. While you won't need to spend money on getting your books published, it takes a considerable amount of time to publish a successful book.

Anyone can write a book and publish it, but if you want to make money, you need to take the time to properly market, promote, and create the content. It can take months to complete a book, and if you do not have an email list, it can be hard to get enough people interested in purchasing your book.

Low-Content Books

If writing a full eBook sounds like too much work or you don't have the time to commit to a big project like a complete manuscript, you can still take advantage of publishing on Amazon with low-content books. Think journals, coloring books, trackers, calendars. These books require minimal writing on your part. You still use Kindle Direct Publish, but you use their print-on-demand feature with published paperback books.

Ideas

You can find low-content books just about anywhere. These include:

- Blank journals
- Prompted journals
- Habit trackers (food, exercise, meditation, gratitude)
- Activity books
- Coloring books
- Recipe books
- Guest books (for wedding, birthday, anniversaries)

You can create one template for a lined journal, change the cover design, and have an unlimited number of low-content books for sale in a short time. You can also create a blank-lined journal with a simple heading at the top of the page, for example: "Today I am grateful for..." These journals are just one of the many ways you can create a book with the same interior and use it repeatedly.

Unlike the cover for eBooks, the cover design for these low-content books can be just about anything. Use a simple image and change the background cover, add a famous inspiration quote, create a pattern, or just add a bunch of different shapes. You can make these covers using popular websites like Canva. If you are publishing an eBook, these low-content books can be a great addition that allows you to bundle the two together and increase your profits.

You can also do this with products you may have up for sale, though this does take some out-of-the-box thinking. For example, if you are selling sheets or coffee mugs, create a gratitude journal and encourage buyers to relax under their sheets or with a cup of coffee while counting their blessings for the day. If you are selling bakeware, include a blank recipe book where buyers can keep their favorite recipes.

Creating Low-Content Books

First, decide the size of your book: 6X9 in., 8x10 in., or 8.5x 11 in. Keep in mind, you can also make your low-content book available as a digital download, and the standard size for these types of printable is 8.5X11 in.

Decide if the content in your book will go all the way to the edges or to stop centered on the page. If you plan to have designs on the interior of your book, you might want these to spill over to the edge of the page. In this case, you would like to choose bleed on. The no bleed option will frame your design with a white border. Decide this early on; with bleed on you need to add .125 in. to the width of your book and .24 in. to the height. For example, if you are going with an 8.5X11 trim, you need to adjust it to 8.625X11.25 in.

Adding color to the interior of your books increases the price you need to sell them at. This may seem like an appealing idea because a higher price means bigger profits but consider that many of the best selling low-content books are typically priced around seven to nine dollars. These books tend to bring in a profit of just three dollars, and you also benefit from using the expanded distribution feature. When you add color to the exterior, this can bump up your sale price to over $13.00, and you would not receive any royalties per sale. To obtain the same profits, you would need to increase your price to over $18.00, and at this price point, you would not be able to use expanded distribution. To use expanded distribution, you would need to sell your low-content book for at least $20.00. At this price, your book will most likely not sell. While the color interior will make your designs look nicer, going with grayscale will improve your chances of making a profit.

With these in mind, you can create your low-content books, as mentioned using Canva for the cover design. You can also use:

- Google Slides
- PowerPoint
- Microsoft Word
- InDesign

You can use these programs to design the cover and lined pages for the interior. You will need to add the lines to your pages; Amazon will not automatically print your books with lined pages. This is easily done by adding a table to a blank page with your desired number of rows, usually around 24. Once you have your table added, delete the outside borders, which will leave only the lines on the page. When you have this done for one page, duplicate the page for how many pages you want your finished journal to have, for example, 100 pages.

Not all books need lined pages. You can promote your low-content book as a sketch pad, in which case you will still need to use one of these programs to create your book, but you will just create a document that contains the blank pages.

This process can be made even simpler by signing up for a site that helps you design low-content books from start to finish for a low monthly fee, such as Book Bolt and Interior Builder. These will streamline the process and tend to cost under $10 a month.

Pros and Cons

With this option, you can quickly get a wider variety of books published, and you do not have to worry about keeping an inventory. There are no upfront investments you need to make either.

It does take some time to get the correct formatting and learning how to keyword your books, so they get found easily, other than that, there is no additional investment needed. With the ability to use the same interior designs for multiple books, you don't have to create each book from beginning to end.

The only con with this option is it can be a highly competitive category to generate sales in. With the right keyword, you can get your book noticed. Target specific audiences, such as dog lovers for books that feature a dog on them. This option is best to sell many different designs to increase the chances of making a substantial profit.

Chapter 5: Digital Goods

We are not referring to just eBooks and courses. There are many ways you can create digital products that generate a steady stream of income. Vector art is one of the most popular forms of digital goods. These can be sold on many design sites like Canva or even Design Space (a cutting machine program for Cricut users). As you will learn, you can find many ways to create digital products and enjoy a steady income stream from very little time or financial investments.

Printables

Many printables can mimic low-content books. You do not need to worry about the printing cost for printing in color; you can make these stand out with lots of colors and details. You will not need to add blank pages for printables. Instead, you can create a full-page layout that the customer can then download and print as many as they need. Printables can include a wide range of items such as:

- Habit trackers
- Calendars
- Social media templates
- Checklists
- Coloring pages
- Worksheets
- Schedules
- Games

These can be easily created using Canva. You can sell each page individually or create a bundle to sell multiple templates together. Printables can be sold through your own website or you can make an Etsy shop. Creative Market is another site that will allow you to sell printables.

Apps

You do not need coding experience to create an app. Online services like BuildFire helps create mobile apps for you or through one of their templates. Apps can generate income through in-app ads, affiliate links, or by charging a download fee. Besides having to do minor updates or adding new features once you have your app created, there is little time spent maintaining this income stream. If you have a blog, you can create an app that provides readers instant access to specific content. For example, if you blog about cooking, you can create a recipe app.

Photography/Video Presets

Photo and video presets are used by everyone. These add special lighting, effects, colors, and more to images and videos. Thanks to social media, these have become high demand. Filters, stickers, and themes can be created and sold through your website or places like Creative Market, FilterGrade, and Behance. You can create presets using popular video and photo software like Adobe Lightroom and Premiere, Final Cut Pro, and DaVinci.

If you have any of these editing programs, you can create a preset package that can build you a sizable side income. Making minor adjustments to the presets you create can offer a wider selection for users and requires little time. When you sell your presets, you want to give users a view of how the presets will affect their images. Creating before and after photos will help users see what they are getting. You can use your social media accounts to start marketing and promote your presets using them on the images and videos you share.

Photography

Stock photography is always in demand. If you have any photography skills, there are plenty of stock photo websites you can sell your images to. Stock photos are used for blogs, advertising, and much more.

You do not need to have an expensive camera. Many people have been able to use their smartphones to take a variety of stock photos. You can also set up a subscription service that allows people to use the images you take for a small monthly fee. The most popular stock photography sites are Adobe Stock, iStock, Shutterstock, and Getty Images.

While this is a passive income, those who create a steady income are constantly adding to their online gallery. Many stock sites have specific requirements images need to meet before making them available on their sites.

Setting Up an Ecommerce

You can set up a digital store and begin uploading your products quickly. The most popular sites include:

- Etsy
- Shopify
- Facebook
- Personal/Business Blog (Woocommerce)
- BigCommerce

Many of these charge a small listing fee for each product you list. Having a solid description of the product is essential. Use keywords that describe your product and terms people are using when searching for similar products. This will get your item found more quickly, even when just starting.

Chapter 6: Trading and Investing

Many shy away from investing and trading as a passive income because it can be a complex process if you don't know where to start. Learn how to get into trading and investing to put away more for retirement, vacations, or add to your current income. Trading and investing can be as passive or active as you desire. Those who are more involved can make a substantial amount of money daily. A more passive approach may take longer to build up, but requires less effort. Keep in mind; there is always a risk when it comes to trading and investing. A general rule with this passive income is never to invest money that you do not intend to lose.

Real Estate Investments Trusts

Real estate investment trusts (REIT) allow you to make money from real estate without owning property or handling the maintenance and additional tenant complaints from owning a physical piece of property. You can invest in apartment complexes, facilities, hotels, retail centers, and many other commercial properties with REITs. You then get paid a dividend on your investment and these can be traded just like any traditional stock. REITs fall into three categories:

- Equity - These are the most common and largest categories. Equity REITs are properties where the income is generated through rental payments.
- Mortgage - Mortgage REITs generate income through a net interest margin because they are loans or mortgage agreements.
- Hybrid - Hybrid REITs have components of both equity and mortgage REITs. There is income-producing property and loans or mortgage agreements on those properties that bring in a stream of income for both avenues.

To get started, you can begin to invest as little as $500; sites like Realty Mogul, Fundrise, and Steitwise allow you to invest in real estate quickly and easily.

REITs offer a long-term income stream. They can be easy to buy and trade, but you will want to do your research before deciding which REIT to buy into. REITs are registered with the Securities and Exchange Commission (SEC). You can verify this by searching the SECs EDGAR system, which will also provide you with annual and quarterly reports of available REITs (Chen, 2020).

Keep in mind that any money you make from a REIT investment will be taxed as a regular income. REITs can also have high transaction fees.

Exchange-Traded Funds

Exchange-traded funds (ETF) offer the best of stock trading and mutual funds. These funds allow you to buy and sell a bundle of assets throughout the trading day. They often have lower fees, and many carry lower risks. Instead of investing in a single stock, you are investing in a more diversified basket of stocks. For example, SPY is a bundle of stocks that follow the S&P 500, HACK is a bundle of cyber security funds, and FONE has a bundle of options that focus on smartphone funds (Voigt, 2021).

ETFs are a standard option for many online brokers. The most common types include (Voigt, 2021):

- Stock ETFs are less risky and are ideal for long-term returns.
- Commodity ETFs are related to raw goods such as coffee or oil. These funds can vary greatly, and you want to know where you are investing in the physical stockpile of the item or companies that produce the product. These funds can have higher risk levels and are subject to different tax regulations.

- Bond ETFs are low-risk investments that do not have a maturity date like traditional bonds. These generate regular cash payments.
- International ETFs focus on foreign investments, which can include investing in an individual country or country blocs.
- Sector ETFs allow you to invest in companies in one of the eleven stock market sectors. These include health care, industrial, and financial sectors. These carry less risk than investing in a single company that falls into one of these sectors. You can track specific business cycles and make a well-rounded judgment of which sector is best to invest in.

Dividend Stocks

Dividend stocks are investments in a company that allow you to reap the benefits from a company's profits. Payments are made on a monthly, quarterly, or yearly schedule. You can use this payout to reinvest and buy more shares of that company. Investing in dividend stocks can be done through many online brokerages without the need for a financial advisor.

There are a few restrictions that may apply to dividend stocks. Some companies only allow you to buy shares of the company if you are an employee or already own the stock. There are limitations to how you can buy or sell your company's shares, reducing the freedom you have with this investment.

When looking for dividend stocks to invest in, consider the following:

- Look at the company's return on equity. This number gives you an estimate of the company's net income and how much dividends are paid out to shareholders.
- How much debt does the company have? A company with a high debt-to-equity ratio will have to spend more money paying off these debts and less going to shareholders.

- Does the company have a steady and increasing profit margin? A company with a growing profit margin over the years will be in a good financial position to pay out dividends, while a decreasing profit margin will struggle to pay investors.
- Choose companies that have been publicly traded for at least 10 years.
- Find undervalued stocks. These are companies selling at lower than they are worth, meaning you can buy into them at a low rate and reap the rewards later. Undervalued stocks are due to the market overreacting, which can be a good time to invest.

Dividend stocks are genuinely passive income. Aside from monitoring how your stock is doing, once you have invested in the stock, there is not much else you need to do. If you set up a dividend reinvestment plan (DRIP), earnings are automatically reinvested into that company.

While this is a highly appealing investment opportunity that can benefit you long-term, there are no guarantees when investing. A company may go out of business or completely stop paying dividends at any time.

Chapter 7: Rent Your Space

Having a rental property has been the most common steady income stream for a long time. Although this is still a favorable income opportunity, owning an apartment or secondary home to rent is not the most financially suitable way to take advantage of rental spaces. Even renting out a spare bedroom and taking in a roommate does not always result in the best situations. Thanks to rental sites like Airbnb, it has become easier to rent out your spare rooms for a short period.

Rental Property

Rental properties have been a long-time safer option for creating a passive income. These, however, require a substantial upfront investment. Even if you have the money to purchase a rental property, you also need to consider the maintenance and emergency expenses. You can get an estimate of these maintenance fees by calculating one percent of the property value (Dillon, 2018). Consider also that you might not always have the most responsible tenants, which can cost you thousands of dollars and added stress.

If you already own a rental property, renting out rooms instead of the entire property can bring you in a little extra income for no more effort. For example, if you have a single-family three-bedroom home that you typically rent out to one family for $1500 a month, you can rent each room to different tenants for $600 to $700 a month. You would bring in an additional $300 to $600 a month. Each tenant would be responsible for their own portion of the rent and would have their personal space with the ability to share common spaces like the living room, kitchen, bathrooms, and outdoor areas.

Renting Your Spare Room

Listing your room for rent on sites like Airbnb has its pros and cons as well. You get your listing exposed to a wide range of travelers. You only have to worry about blocking out certain days when guests will be staying there. For the most part, those who use these services understand that it is your home, and are more respectful of the space. This is not for every person, but it is a general rule. The other nice thing about renting space on Airbnb is that the people looking for a room to stay in, are typically not going to be there the entire time. Many people are just looking for a place to sleep that is cheaper than most hotel rooms.

There are additional perks to offering your spare room for rent on Airbnb. If you become a Superhost, you can get extra freebies. A Superhost has phenomenal reviews and meets other requirements, like hosting for at least a year, quick response time, and one cancellation for every 100 booked. Many companies offer hosts free samples, from toiletries to mattresses, sheets, and pillows. On top of this, you can get a $100 freebie bonus from Airbnb.

Choosing the right price for your listing can be done in a few ways. First, decide how many days you are willing to rent your spare space, then determine your monthly fees if you were just renting out this room to a traditional tenant. Divide your monthly expenses by the days you are willing to rent out your room, and you will get an estimate of how much you want to rent your space for. If, however, you only want to rent your area a few times a month, this will give you a high price that will not get your space rented out. Instead, look at what similar listings are charging, then divide your total expense by 30. This will give you the minimum you want to charge per night, whether you are only renting for a few days each month or most of the month. Also, consider that you will need to clean the space after each guest. You can add cleaning fees in addition to the nightly fees. This helps cover the cost of cleaning materials, laundry, and the time you need to spend doing the cleaning.

This is a good option for those who have a spare room that is not being used. All you need to do is take quality images of your space and get it listed on Airbnb. Then you just have to worry about the cleaning and staying up to date with bookings, such as messaging potential guests and verifying their identity. Though this can be a passive income, there is no guarantee that you will be booked as much as you would like. This means you can't always be sure how much you will earn in a month, especially at the beginning.

Conclusion

It doesn't matter what age you are; whether you just graduated college or are nearing retirement, a passive income is essential. The right passive income can complement your current earnings or replace them. It gives you financial security for the future and allows you to explore entrepreneurship without most of the major risks.

This book has provided you with various passive income options and easy to get started steps. You have learned the pros and cons of each possibility to decide which one works with your current lifestyle. You can use these suggestions to build a more complex stream of income if you choose. A passive income often begins as a hobby that stems from a passion. This passion drives many people to establish a profitable business where they have more control over their earnings and the hours they work.

A passive income is easy to get started on; though the beginning may take slightly more time to begin seeing a steady income, it is well worth it. You can begin to generate an income in your spare time while working a full-time job or taking care of the kids. Now that you know how, all you need to do is take action and get started!

If you enjoyed this book in anyway, an honest review is always appreciated!

References

Awosika, A. (2021, April 22). *How to make money with Kindle Direct Publishing [case study].* Smart Blogger. https://smartblogger.com/kindle-publishing/

Brown, A. G. (2018, March 27). *How to make and sell your own Lightroom presets.* Format. https://www.format.com/magazine/resources/photography/how-to-make-and-sell-lightroom-presets

Chen, J. (2020, June 30). *Owning property via a real estate investment trust.* Investopedia. https://www.investopedia.com/terms/r/reit.asp

Connolly, A. (2021, January 17). *How much money do Amazon sellers make?* Jungle Scout. https://www.junglescout.com/blog/how-much-money-amazon-sellers-make/

Darko. (2020, February 19). *19 amazing MLM statistics you should read in 2020.* Jobs In Marketing. https://jobsinmarketing.io/blog/mlm-statistics/

Dillon, M. (2018, June 23). *How much should a landlord allocate for monthly maintenance & repairs.* SFGate. https://homeguides.sfgate.com/much-should-landlord-allocate-monthly-maintenance-repairs-80019.html

Enfroy, A. (n.d.). *Affiliate marketing in 2020: what it is and how beginners can start.* The BigCommerce Blog. https://www.bigcommerce.com/blog/affiliate-marketing/#how-do-affiliate-marketers-get-paid

Ferreira, C. (2021a, January 1). *How to find and work with reliable dropshipping suppliers.* Shopify. https://www.shopify.com/blog/dropshipping-suppliers

Ferreira, C. (2021b, January 2). *how to start a dropshipping business: A complete playbook for 2021.* Shopify.

https://www.shopify.com/blog/how-to-start-dropshipping#:~:text=How%20much%20can%20you%20make

Hayes, A. (2021, March 16). *Network marketing.* Investopedia. https://www.investopedia.com/terms/n/network-marketing.asp

Kevin. (2021, January 11). *Making money with Airbnb in 2021: Why I rent out our guest room.* Financial Panther. https://financialpanther.com/making-money-airbnb-rent-guest-room/

Lake, R. (2019, October 27). *Make money with affiliate marketing.* Investopedia. https://www.investopedia.com/personal-finance/affiliate-marketing-can-you-really-make-money/#:~:text=According%20to%20the%20survey%2C%209

Patel, N. (n.d.). *How to start a blog that generates $3817 a month.* Neil Patel. https://neilpatel.com/how-to-start-a-blog/#step-10

Roach, A. (2021, March 19). *How to find the perfect dropshipping products.* Oberlo Dropshipping app. https://www.oberlo.com/blog/find-perfect-dropshipping-products

Sheehan, A. (2019, March 14). *How much to charge for your Airbnb rental.* Money under 30. https://www.moneyunder30.com/how-much-to-charge-for-airbnb

Thackston, K. (2020, February 22). *The power & profits of low-content Amazon self-publishing (no inventory!).* Marketing Words. https://www.marketingwords.com/blog/amazon-self-publishing/

Voigt, K. (2021, April 26). *What is an etf? a beginner's complete guide.* NerdWallet. https://www.nerdwallet.com/article/investing/what-is-an-etf

WPBeginner Editorial Staff. (2020, January 2). *How to start a podcast (and make it successful) in 2020.* WPBeginner. https://www.wpbeginner.com/wp-tutorials/step-by-step-guide-how-to-start-a-podcast-with-wordpress/